Newmark LEARNING

3

Common Core

Reading

Warm-Ups & Test Practice

Newmark Learning
145 Huguenot Street • New Rochelle, NY 10801

Editor: Ellen Ungaro
Designer: Raquel Hernández

Photo credits: Page 33: Courtesy of NASA; Page 43: Associated Press; Page 93: Courtesy of Library of Congress

Table of Contents

Introduction

What are the new Common Core assessments?

The Common Core State Standards for English Language Arts have set shared, consistent, and clear objectives of what students are expected to learn. The standards are intended to be rigorous and reflect what students will need to be able to do to be college and career ready by the end of high school.

As a part of this initiative, two consortia of states, the Partnership for Assessment of Readiness for College and Careers (PARCC) and Smarter Balanced, have developed new assessments that are aligned with the Common Core State Standards and designed to measure students' progress toward college and career readiness.

How are the new assessments different?

The new standardized assessments from both PARCC and Smarter Balanced are designed to be taken online and include many new types of assessment items.

In addition to multiple-choice questions, the assessments include both short and extended constructed-response questions, which require students to develop written responses that include examples and details from the text.

Another key element in the PARCC and Smarter Balanced assessments is the two-part question. In two-part questions, Part B asks students to identify the text evidence that supports their answer to Part A. These questions reflect the new emphasis on text evidence in the Common Core Standards. Anchor Standard 1 for Reading states that students should "cite specific textual evidence when writing or speaking to support conclusions drawn from the text."

The assessments from PARCC and Smarter Balanced also include technology-enhanced questions. These items, which students will encounter if they take the online assessments, ask students to interact with and manipulate text. For example, some questions ask students to select two or three correct answers from a list. Other questions ask students to identify important events in a story and then arrange them in the correct order.

The assessments from PARCC and Smarter Balanced will also feature passages that meet the requirements for complex texts set by the Common Core State Standards. The ability to read and comprehend complex text is another key element of the new standards. Anchor Standard 10 for reading states that students should be able to "Read and comprehend complex literary and informational texts independently and proficiently."

Common Core Reading Warm-Ups & Test Practice is designed to help prepare students for these new assessments from PARCC and Smarter Balanced. The Warm Ups and Practice Tests will help students rehearse the kind of thinking needed for success on the online assessments.

What Test Will Your State Take?

Smarter Balanced States	PARCC States
Alaska	Arizona
California	Arkansas
Connecticut	Colorado
Delaware	District of Columbia
Hawaii	
Idaho	Florida
Iowa	Georgia
Kansas	Illinois
Maine	Indiana
Michigan	Kentucky
Missouri	Louisiana
Montana	Maryland
Nevada	Massachusetts
New Hampshire	Mississippi
North Carolina	New Jersey
North Dakota	New Mexico
Oregon	New York
Pennsylvania	North Dakota
South Carolina	Ohio
South Dakota	Oklahoma
U.S. Virgin Islands	Pennsylvania
Vermont	Rhode Island
Washington	Tennessee
West Virginia	
Wisconsin	
Wyoming	

How will this book help students prepare?

Warm Ups for Guided Practice

Common Core Reading Warm-Ups and Test Practice include ten Warm Ups, which are short tests that are designed to provide students with an opportunity for quick, guided practice.

The ten Warm Ups feature short reading passages that include examples of the genres that students are required to read in each grade level and will encounter on the test. In grade 3, the Common Core State Standards require students to read folktales, fables, drama, poetry, social studies, science, and technical texts.

Fairy Tale

Poetry

Science Text

Technical/How-to

The questions that follow the Warm Ups include the variety of formats and question types that students will encounter on the new assessments. They include two-part questions, constructed response (short answer) questions, and questions that replicate the technology-enhanced items.

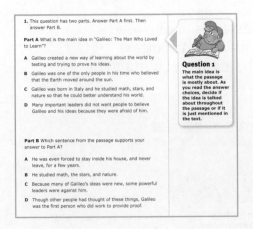

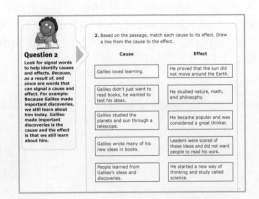

The Warm Ups also include prompts with each question. These prompts are designed to guide students through the test. They model the thinking needed for answering questions, provide reading strategies, and include additional support for answering the questions.

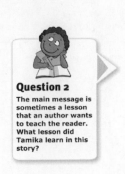

Question 2
The main message is sometimes a lesson that an author wants to teach the reader. What lesson did Tamika learn in this story?

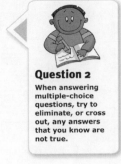

Question 2
When answering multiple-choice questions, try to eliminate, or cross out, any answers that you know are not true.

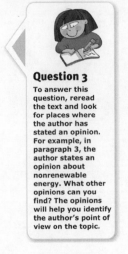

Question 3
To answer this question, reread the text and look for places where the author has stated an opinion. For example, in paragraph 3, the author states an opinion about nonrenewable energy. What other opinions can you find? The opinions will help you identify the author's point of view on the topic.

Practice Tests to Build Test-Taking Stamina

The Practice Tests feature longer passages that match the passage lengths that will be used for the PARCC and Smarter Balanced tests. These passages provide students with experience reading the longer and more complex texts they will have to read on the new assessments.

Two of the Practice Tests also feature paired passages. The paired passages give students the opportunity to compare and contrast texts and integrate information from multiple texts, as required by Standard R.9.

Literature

Informational Texts

Paired Texts

Each passage is followed by a complete set of questions that reflect the number of questions students will find with each passage on the new assessments. In addition, similar to the Warm Ups, the Practice Tests also include the types of questions students will see on the new assessments, including two-part questions and questions that model the technology-enhanced items. Every Practice Test also includes three constructed response (short answer) questions to give students practice writing about texts and using details from the text in their response.

2. This question has two parts. Answer Part A first. Then answer Part B.

Part A Read this sentence from the passage.

People lived all crammed together in a loud, <u>bustling</u>, tall city.

What is the meaning of the word <u>bustling</u>?

A   noisy

B   busy

C   large

D   boring

Part B Choose two phrases from the passage that help you understand the meaning of the word <u>bustling</u>.

A   all crammed together

B   driving about

C   rush all the time

D   red, green, yellow

E   colorful pictures

Two-part questions

4. How does Palma change by the end of the story? Check the box for the three details that tell what she is like at the end.

☐ She no longer misses her village in the Philippines.

☐ She has learned to accept the idea of snow.

☐ She will make the best of her new home for the sake of her family.

☐ She is going to forget about her friends back in the Philippines.

☐ She will stop watching movies on TV and start playing outside more.

☐ She realizes that things that seem strange at first can also be beautiful.

Questions with multiple answers

8. Why did Palma's aunt mention Mulan to her? Use details from the passage to support your answer.

_____
_____
_____
_____
_____
_____
_____
_____

9. As the snow is falling, what does Auntie see when she looks at Palma? Describe Palma at that moment from Auntie's point of view. Include at least two details from the passage.

_____
_____
_____
_____
_____

10. What lesson does Palma learn in this story, and how does she learn it? Use at least three details from the passage to support your answer.

_____
_____
_____
_____
_____
_____
_____
_____
_____
_____
_____
_____
_____

Constructed-response questions

Correlated to the Common Core State Standards

All of the assessment items are correlated to the Reading Standards for Literature or the Reading Standards for Informational Text. The correlation chart below shows the standards that each Warm Up and Practice Test addresses.

TEST	RL/RI 3.1	RL/RI 3.2	RL/RI 3.3	RL/RI 3.4	RL/RI 3.5	RL/RI 3.6	RL/RI 3.7	RL/RI 3.8	RL/RI 3.9
Warm Up 1	X	X	X	X					
Warm Up 2		X	X				X		
Warm Up 3		X		X	X				
Warm Up 4	X	X		X					
Warm Up 5	X		X	X					
Warm Up 6	X	X		X		X			
Warm Up 7	X	X	X				X		
Warm Up 8	X	X				X			
Warm Up 9		X		X		X			
Warm Up 10		X	X	X		X			
Practice Test 1	X	X	X	X	X	X			
Practice Test 2	X	X	X	X	X	X	X		
Practice Test 3	X	X	X	X	X		X		X
Practice Test 4	X	X	X	X		X		X	

Grade 3 Common Core State Standards

Reading Standards for Literature

RL.3.1 Ask and answer questions to demonstrate understanding of a text, referring explicitly to the text as the basis for the answers.

RL.3.2 Recount stories, including fables, folktales, and myths from diverse cultures; determine the central message, lesson, or moral and explain how it is conveyed through key details in the text.

RL.3.3 Describe characters in a story (e.g., their traits, motivations, or feelings) and explain how their actions contribute to the sequence of events.

RL.3.4 Determine the meaning of words and phrases as they are used in a text, distinguishing literal from nonliteral language.

RL.3.5 Refer to parts of stories, dramas, and poems when writing or speaking about a text, using terms such as *chapter, scene,* and *stanza*; describe how each successive part builds on earlier sections.

RL.3.6 Distinguish their own point of view from that of the narrator or those of the characters.

RL.3.7 Explain how specific aspects of a text's illustrations contribute to what is conveyed by the words in a story (e.g., create mood, emphasize aspects of a character or setting).

RL.3.9 Compare and contrast the themes, settings, and plots of stories written by the same author about the same or similar characters (e.g., in books from a series).

Reading Standards for Informational Texts

RI.3.1 Ask and answer questions to demonstrate understanding of a text, referring explicitly to the text as the basis for the answers.

RI.3.2 Determine the main idea of a text; recount the key details and explain how they support the main idea.

RI.3.3 Describe the relationship between a series of historical events, scientific ideas or concepts, or steps in technical procedures in a text, using language that pertains to time, sequence, and cause/effect.

RI.3.4 Determine the meaning of general academic and domain-specific words and phrases in a text relevant to a grade 3 topic or subject area.

RI.3.5 Use text features and search tools (e.g., key words, sidebars, hyperlinks) to locate information relevant to a given topic efficiently.

RI.3.6 Distinguish their own point of view from that of the author of a text.

RI.3.7 Use information gained from illustrations (e.g., maps, photographs) and the words in a text to demonstrate understanding of the text (e.g., where, when, why, and how key events occur).

RI.3.8 Describe the logical connection between particular sentences and paragraphs in a text (e.g., comparison, cause/effect, first/second/third in a sequence).

RI.3.9 Compare and contrast the most important points and key details presented in two texts on the same topic.

How to Use Common Core Reading Warm Ups and Practice Tests

The Warm Ups are designed to be quick and easy practice for students. They can be used in a variety of ways:

- Assign Warm Ups for homework.

- Use them for quick review in class.

- Use them for targeted review of key standards. The correlation chart on page 10 can help identify Warm Ups that address the skills you want to focus on.

The longer Practice Tests can be used to prepare students in the weeks before the assessments. They can also be used to help assess students' reading comprehension throughout the year.

Tear-out Answer Keys

Find the answers to all the Warm Ups and Practice Tests in the Answer Key beginning on page 103. The Answer Key includes the standards correlations for each question. In addition, it includes sample answers for the constructed response (short answer) questions.

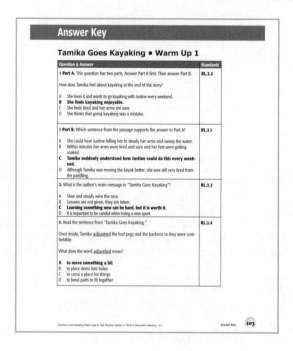

Common Core ELA STANDARDS

RL.3.1
Ask and answer questions to demonstrate understanding of a text, referring explicitly to the text as the basis for the answers.

RL.3.2
Recount stories, including fables, folktales, and myths from diverse cultures; determine the central message, lesson, or moral and explain how it is conveyed through key details in the text.

RL.3.3
Describe characters in a story (e.g., their traits, motivations, or feelings) and explain how their actions contribute to the sequence of events.

RL.3.4
Determine the meaning of words and phrases as they are used in a text, distinguishing literal from nonliteral language.

Read this passage and then answer the questions that follow.

Tamika Goes Kayaking

1   Tamika put on her life jacket and tightened the strap on her helmet. *This is it,* she thought. *I am as ready as I can be.*

2   Tamika smiled as the man from the kayak rental shop showed her the kayaks by the riverbank. As she stepped into the shiny blue kayak, she tried to stop worrying. *I hope I don't tip over the kayak. I don't want to get soaking wet before I even start,* Tamika said to herself.

3   Once inside, Tamika adjusted the foot pegs and the backrest so they were comfortable. The man from the shop handed her the paddle and gave her a little push into the water. He smiled and waved. "Have fun! See you in two hours!" he called to her.

continued ➤

4   Tamika held the paddle and began digging it into the water. Within minutes her arms were tired and sore and her feet were getting soaked. Worse, she hadn't gone very far. Kayaking was starting to seem like a mistake. Suddenly Tamika had an idea; what if she turned the paddle over? She tried it and was soon moving through the water.

5   Although Tamika was moving the kayak better, she was still very tired from the paddling. It was hard to imagine people doing this for hours. Tamika tried to think of the tips she had heard from her friend, Justine, who loved kayaking. She could hear Justine telling her to steady her arms and sweep the water. So Tamika did that, and it worked. Tamika began gliding through the water. As she floated down the river, she noticed what a beautiful day it was. The air felt clean and crisp and the sky was a bright blue. Floating along on the slowly flowing river was very calming. Tamika suddenly understood how Justine could do this every weekend.

Name_____ Date_____

1. This question has two parts. Answer Part A first. Then answer Part B.

Part A How does Tamika feel about kayaking at the end of the story?

A She wants to buy a kayak and go kayaking with Justine every weekend.

B She finds kayaking enjoyable.

C She feels tired and her arms are sore.

D She thinks that going kayaking was a mistake.

Part B Which sentence from the passage supports the answer to Part A?

A She could hear Justine telling her to steady her arms and sweep the water.

B Within minutes her arms were tired and sore and her feet were getting soaked.

C Tamika suddenly understood how Justine could do this every weekend.

D Although Tamika was moving the kayak better, she was still very tired from the paddling.

Question 1

This question asks how Tamika feels about kayaking at the end of the story. Reread paragraph 5 and look for descriptive details that tell you what Tamika is thinking about and how she is feeling.

continued

Name_____ Date_____

Question 2

The main message is sometimes a lesson that an author wants to teach the reader. What lesson did Tamika learn in this story?

Question 3

To understand the meaning of an unfamiliar word, look for clues in the text around the word. In this sentence, the clue is that Tamika adjusted something to make it more comfortable.

2. What is the author's main message in "Tamika Goes Kayaking"?

A Slow and steady wins the race.

B Lessons are not given; they are taken.

C Learning something new can be hard, but it is worth it.

D It is important to be careful when trying a new sport.

3. Read the sentence from "Tamika Goes Kayaking."

Once inside, Tamika <u>adjusted</u> the foot pegs and the backrest so they were comfortable.

What does the word <u>adjusted</u> mean?

A to move something a bit

B to place items into holes

C to carve a place for things

D to bend parts to fit together

RI.3.2
Determine the main idea of a text; recount the key details and explain how they support the main idea.

RI.3.3
Describe the relationship between a series of historical events, scientific ideas or concepts, or steps in technical procedures in a text, using language that pertains to time, sequence, and cause/effect.

RI.3.7
Use information gained from illustrations (e.g., maps, photographs) and the words in a text to demonstrate understanding of the text (e.g., where, when, why, and how key events occur).

Read this passage and then answer the questions that follow.

Galileo: The Man Who Loved to Learn

1   Galileo Galilei was a great thinker and scientist. Although he was born in sixteenth-century Italy, Galileo made contributions to science that are still important today.

2   Galileo loved to learn. He studied math, the stars, and nature. He even studied philosophy—ideas about how people should live. Before Galileo's time, people investigated similar things, but not in the same way. Galileo is said to be the first person in history to really "do" science. He did experiments and hands-on tests to try to prove his ideas. He tried and tried again until he better understood what he was examining. This work paved the way for a whole new field of study that, today, is called science.

continued ►

3   Galileo was interested in learning about the planets and the stars. He built a telescope so he could study them. As a result, he saw that the sun didn't move around the Earth, as most people believed. Actually, the opposite was true: the Earth moved around the sun. Though other people had thought of these things, Galileo was the first person who did work to provide proof.

4   Galileo was also a writer. He wrote his thoughts and discoveries in books. Because many of Galileo's ideas were new, some powerful leaders were against him. Galileo's findings about the Earth's movement upset them most. These leaders were afraid of how their understanding of the world might be different if Galileo was right. So, for a while, Galileo's books were banned in his country. He was even forced to stay inside his house, and never leave, for a few years.

5   Although some people did not like Galileo, many did. He became popular quickly as his readers learned from his ideas and ways of studying things. Today, four hundred years later, Galileo is still loved and remembered. He paved the way for science to become a method of learning. He was brave enough to continue, no matter how tough things were.

Galileo's Inventions

Invention	Uses
Telescope	In 1609, Galileo built his own version of a telescope. He was the first to use a telescope to look at and study the universe.
Geometric Compass	Galileo invented a compass, an instrument used to measure distances, in 1597.
Water Pump	In 1594, Galileo received a patent for his invention of a pump that could be used to collect water.

Name_____ Date_____

1. This question has two parts. Answer Part A first. Then answer Part B.

Part A What is the main idea in "Galileo: The Man Who Loved to Learn"?

A Galileo created a new way of learning about the world by testing and trying to prove his ideas.

B Galileo was one of the only people in his time who believed that the Earth moved around the sun.

C Galileo was born in Italy and he studied math, stars, and nature so that he could better understand his world.

D Many important leaders did not want people to believe Galileo and his ideas because they were afraid of him.

Question 1
The main idea is what the passage is mostly about. As you read the answer choices, decide if the idea is talked about throughout the passage or if it is just mentioned in the text.

Part B Which sentence from the passage supports your answer to Part A?

A He was even forced to stay inside his house, and never leave, for a few years.

B He studied math, the stars, and nature.

C Because many of Galileo's ideas were new, some powerful leaders were against him.

D Though other people had thought of these things, Galileo was the first person who did work to provide proof.

continued →

Name_____ Date_____

Question 2

Look for signal words to help identify causes and effects. *Because*, *as a result of*, and *since* are words that can signal a cause and effect. For example: Because Galileo made important discoveries, we still learn about him today. Galileo made important discoveries is the cause and the effect is that we still learn about him.

Question 3

It is important to pay careful attention to charts, diagrams, and illustrations that are included in passages. They often include additional information that is not in the passage. The chart included in this passage adds new information about the tools that Galileo invented.

2. Based on the passage, match each cause to its effect. Draw a line from the cause to the effect.

Cause	Effect
Galileo loved learning.	He proved that the sun did not move around the Earth.
Galileo didn't just want to read books; he wanted to test his ideas.	He studied nature, math, and philosophy.
Galileo studied the planets and sun through a telescope.	He became popular and was considered a great thinker.
Galileo wrote many of his new ideas in books.	Leaders were scared of these ideas and did not want people to read his work.
People learned from Galileo's ideas and discoveries.	He started a new way of thinking and study called science.

3. Using the information from the chart and the passage, what inference can you make about Galileo's inventions?

A He created tools that could help him do hands-on tests.

B He was mostly interested in space and how the planets moved.

C He read every book on a subject before forming a new thought.

D He was more interested in inventing new tools.

STOP!

ommon
ore ELA
STANDARDS

RL.3.2
Recount stories, including fables, folktales, and myths from diverse cultures; determine the central message, lesson, or moral and explain how it is conveyed through key details in the text.

RL.3.4
Determine the meaning of words and phrases as they are used in a text, distinguishing literal from nonliteral language.

RL.3.5
Refer to parts of stories, dramas, and poems when writing or speaking about a text, using terms such as *chapter*, *scene*, and *stanza*; describe how each successive part builds on earlier sections.

Read this passage and then answer the questions that follow.

Tree on the Hill

On yonder hill there stood a tree;

Tree on the hill, and the hill stood still.

And on the tree there was a branch;

Branch on the tree, tree on the hill, and the hill

5   stood still.

And on the branch there was a nest;

Nest on the branch, branch on the tree, tree on

     the hill, and the hill stood still.

continued ➡

And in the nest there was an egg;

10   Egg in the nest, nest on the branch, branch on

       the tree, tree on the hill, and the hill stood

       still.

And in the egg there was a bird;

Bird in the egg, egg in the nest, nest on the

15   branch, branch on the tree, tree on the hill,

       and the hill stood still.

And on the bird there was a feather;

Feather on the bird, bird in the egg, egg in the

       nest, nest on the branch, branch on the tree,

20   tree on the hill, and the hill stood still.

Name_____ Date_____

1. This question has two parts. Answer Part A first. Then answer Part B.

Part A Which of the following best describes the poem's form?

A   Two of the stanzas are the same.

B   The poem uses rhyming in each stanza.

C   The stanzas get longer and build on ideas.

D   Each stanza in the poem has the same number of syllables.

Part B What line might the poet have used to begin a seventh stanza?

A   And in the nest there was a bird

B   And on the twig there was a leaf

C   And on the bird there was a raindrop

D   And on the feather there was a bug

Question 1

Poems are divided into stanzas to make the poem easier to read and understand. Poets use stanzas to separate ideas and thoughts from each other the way authors use paragraphs in their writing.

continued

Name_____ Date_____

Question 2

Giving human traits to animals or objects is called personification. Which of these examples gives a human trait to an animal or an object?

2. In which phrase does the poet talk about an object as if it were a person?

A Bird in the egg, egg in the nest

B Feather on the bird, bird in the egg

C Nest on the branch, branch on the tree

D Tree on the hill, and the hill stood still

Question 3

The central message is the big idea that the author is trying to get across. This poem is about a bird's nest in a tree, but there is a bigger idea that the poet wants to tell the reader.

3. What is the central message in "Tree on the Hill"?

A Birds build their nests in trees.

B Animals with feathers lay eggs.

C Everything in life is connected to something else.

D People should treat trees and animals with respect.

Common Core ELA STANDARDS

RI.3.1
Ask and answer questions to demonstrate understanding of a text, referring explicitly to the text as the basis for the answers.

RI.3.2
Determine the main idea of a text; recount the key details and explain how they support the main idea.

RI.3.4
Determine the meaning of general academic and domain-specific words and phrases in a text relevant to a *grade 3 topic or subject area.*

Read this passage and then answer the questions that follow.

Making Good Use of Garbage

Adapted from Vermicomposting http://kids.niehs.nih.gov/explore/reduce/worms.htm

1   You can recycle many things you use—even garbage!

2   Worms can turn our old food into plant food. It's called vermicomposting.

3   Vermicomposting can be fun, but it is also good for our planet!

continued ➤

Fun Worm Facts!

4   • Red worms may live for up to 4.5 years when they are kept for vermicomposting (compared to 1 year in the wild), and will grow to a length of up to 3 inches.

5   • Red worms can live in a wide range of temperatures. They're happiest from 55°F to 70°F but can handle 45°F to 80°F.

6   • Red worms can reproduce quickly in confinement. Their population may double or triple in 1 year.

How Do You Vermicompost?

7   **Step 1** Make a dark house for the worms to live in. Use a wooden or plastic bin or other nonmetal container. A bin 1.5 feet high by 2 feet deep by 3 feet wide is a good size for a household. Make drain holes near the bottom.

8   **Step 2** Fill the bin with moist bedding. Bedding can be shredded paper or newspaper, leaves, straw, peat moss, or sawdust. Make sure the bedding is kept very moist, like a sponge. Change the bedding once or twice a year.

9   **Step 3** Feed the worms.
     Yes!   Fruit, vegetables, coffee grounds, bread, leaves
     No!   Milk, oil, eggs, meat, fat

10   **Step 4** Dig a hole in the bedding, dump the food in, and cover it up with bedding. Pick a new spot each time you add food.

11   **Step 5** Keep the worms damp and warm. Add water if the bedding feels dry, but make sure that the excess water can drain away. Cover the bin with plastic or a tarp during freezing weather.

Name_____ Date_____

1. This question has two parts. Answer Part A first. Then answer Part B.

Part A What do red worms need to live and grow?

A water pools

B damp bedding

C strong sunlight

D freezing temperatures

Part B Which sentence from the passage supports your answer to Part A?

A Pick a new spot each time you add food.

B Cover the bin with plastic or a tarp during freezing weather.

C Make sure the bedding is kept very moist, like a sponge.

D Use a wooden or plastic bin or other nonmetal container.

Question 1

Informational texts sometimes have subheads that tell you what each section of text is about. Use the subheads when you go back into the text to find answers. For this question, details about what red worms need to live and grow will most likely be found in the section "How Do You Vermicompost?"

continued

Name_____ Date_____

Question 2

A summary is a retelling of the text in a few sentences. When you summarize, you use only the most important details. You can cross out any sentence choices that have details that are not very important and would not be included in a summary.

2. Choose three sentences that would be included in a summary of "Making Good Use of Garbage." Number them in the correct order.

—   You have to change their bedding at least once a year.

—   Worms are very good to use for fishing and are good for the Earth, but they do not live long in the wild.

—   They need to be covered with a tarp during cold weather.

—   Make a box using plastic or wood, but be sure to stay away from metal containers.

—   Vermicomposting is using worms to recycle food waste into plant food.

—   Worms can be fed fruits, vegetables, coffee grounds, and bread, but they should not be fed meat, eggs, or milk.

—   They can live in damp shredded newspaper, sawdust, or leaves.

—   Worms need a warm, dark place with moist bedding and food so that they can grow.

Question 3

For vocabulary questions, reread the sentences in the text around the word, and try to decide what the word means using clues from these sentences. Then check the answer choices and see if one of the choices matches your answer.

3. Read the sentence from "Making Good Use of Garbage."

Their population may double or triple in 1 year.

What is the definition of the word population?

A   the years of life

B   the number of beings

C   the length of something

D   the size of a certain space

STOP!

Read this passage and then answer the questions that follow.

The Princess on the Mountaintop

1   Once upon a time, there was a kind, beautiful princess who lived atop a steep mountain. Gallant young princes would travel from all over the land to ask for her hand in marriage. Yet the princess's castle could not be reached because it was high on a mountaintop. There was no path or roads to get to it. So the princess waited patiently while the princes came and went.

2   A wise old man lived in a shack at the bottom of the mountain. Eager young men often knocked on his door. They asked him how to reach the peak of the mountain. The wise old man would hand them a magical bean and tell them a riddle:

When I'm hot, I rise.

When I'm cold, I fall.

What fills me up most

Is nothing at all.

continued ▶

3   The old man then said that the bean must be planted at night and the answer to the riddle must be spoken out loud by morning. Only the correct answer would get the young man to the top.

4   One day, three young men approached with fanciful dreams of marrying the princess. The old man gave them each a bean, told them the riddle, and sent them on their way. Two of the men planted their beans and went home to sleep. But the third man stayed up all night to ponder the riddle and came up with an answer.

5   In the morning, the beans had sprouted into three different things. The first man's bean turned into a rope, but it was far too short to reach the top of the mountain. The second man's bean turned into a horse, but the horse could not find a path to walk up. The third man's bean turned into a hot air balloon, and he rode it to the top to meet his bride.

Name_____ Date_____

1. This question has two parts. Answer Part A first. Then answer Part B.

Part A Which of the following words best describes the third man?

A lazy

B clever

C selfish

D honest

Part B What sentence from the passage supports your answer to Part A?

A Eager young men often knocked on his door.

B But the third man stayed up all night to ponder the riddle and came up with an answer.

C Only the correct answer would get the young man to the top.

D In the morning, the beans had sprouted into three different things.

Question 1
To describe a character, look at what the character says and does. The first two men plant the bean and then leave. What does the third man do? Which of the answer choices best describes the character?

continued ➡

Name_____ Date_____

Question 2

Some words have multiple meanings. When you find a word with multiple meanings, look carefully at how the word is used in the text. In this case, *peak* is being used to describe part of a mountain.

2. Read the sentence from the passage.

> They asked him how to reach the <u>peak</u> of the mountain.

What does the word <u>peak</u> mean in this sentence?

A a clear path

B a hidden cave

C a pointed top

D a smooth side

Question 3

This question is asking *why* the old wise old man is giving out beans. Reread paragraph 2 to look for the answer to this question or to check your answer.

3. Why did the wise man give out magical beans?

A They were the only way to reach the princess.

B They were a test to see who could answer the riddle.

C They were the prize for a correct answer to the riddle.

D They were food for the hungry men who came from far away.

STOP!

RI.3.1
Ask and answer questions to demonstrate understanding of a text, referring explicitly to the text as the basis for the answers.

RI.3.2
Determine the main idea of a text; recount the key details and explain how they support the main idea.

RI.3.4
Determine the meaning of general academic and domain-specific words and phrases in a text relevant to a *grade 3 topic or subject area.*

RI.3.6
Distinguish their own point of view from that of the author of a text.

Read this passage and then answer the questions that follow.

What Is Pluto?

**Adapted from http://www.nasa.gov/audience/
forstudents/k-4/stories/what-is-pluto-k4.html**

1   Pluto was discovered in 1930 by an astronomer from the United States. An astronomer is a person who studies stars and other objects in space.

2   Pluto has three moons. Its largest moon is named Charon (KAIR-en). Charon is about half the size of Pluto. Pluto's two other moons are named Nix and Hydra. They were discovered in 2005. NASA's Hubble Space Telescope took pictures of the two new moons. Nix and Hydra are very small.

3   Pluto was known as the smallest planet in the solar system and the ninth planet from the sun. But in 2003, an astronomer saw a new object beyond Pluto. The astronomer thought he had found a new planet. The object he saw was larger than Pluto. He named the object Eris (EER-is).

continued ➤

4   Finding Eris caused other astronomers to talk about what makes a planet a "planet." There is a group of astronomers who name objects in space. This group decided that Pluto was not really a planet because of its size and location in space. So Pluto and objects like it are now called "dwarf planets." A dwarf planet orbits the sun just like other planets, but it is smaller. A dwarf planet is so small it cannot clear other objects out of its path.

5   Pluto is also called a "plutoid." A plutoid is a dwarf planet that is farther out in space than the planet Neptune. The three known plutoids are Pluto, Eris, and Makemake (MAH-kee-MAH-kee). Astronomers use telescopes to discover new objects like plutoids.

6   Scientists are learning more about the universe and Earth's place in it. Learning more about faraway objects in the solar system is helping astronomers learn more about what it means to be a planet.

Name_____ Date_____

1. This question has two parts. Answer Part A first. Then answer Part B.

Part A What is the main idea of "What Is Pluto?"

A Pluto is now called a dwarf planet because it is much smaller than other space objects.

B The universe is so huge that astronomers are always finding new planets and moons.

C Scientists are learning more about objects in the universe and what it means to be a planet.

D The dwarf planet Pluto has three moons that have been discovered with telescopes.

Question 1

This question asks you to first identify the main idea. Then in Part B, you have to identify the key details that support the main idea. If the main idea is Answer C, which of the details in Part B give the reader information about how scientists are learning more about objects in the universe?

Part B Which of following details from the text support the main idea? Check the box next to each detail you choose.

☐ Astronomers use telescopes to discover new objects like plutoids.

☐ Pluto has three moons.

☐ Charon is about half the size of Pluto.

☐ In 2003, an astronomer saw a new object beyond Pluto.

☐ Finding Eris caused other astronomers to talk about what makes a planet a "planet."

☐ An astronomer is a person who studies stars and other objects in space.

continued

Name_____ Date_____

Question 2

Authors write for several reasons. They may try to persuade or convince the reader of something. They may write to entertain readers and make them laugh. Or they may write to inform or teach readers about something. Ask yourself why the author wrote this passage.

Question 3

Sometimes clues to a word's definition are not in the same sentence or paragraph. In this example, you can find a clue to the word's meaning in paragraph 5. A plutoid is described as "farther out in space."

2. What is the author's purpose for writing "What Is Pluto?"

A to inform readers about planets and space

B to entertain readers with stories about space

C to persuade readers that Pluto is a dwarf planet

D to convince readers that Eris is the farthest planet

3. Read the sentence from "What Is Pluto?"

> This group decided that Pluto was not really a planet because of its size and <u>location</u> in space.

What does the word <u>location</u> mean?

A path

B time

C place

D color

Name_____ Date_____

4. Explain how a dwarf planet is similar to a planet and how it is different from a planet. Use details from the text to support your answer.

_____

_____

_____

_____

_____

_____

_____

Question 4

Scanning the first sentence of each paragraph is a good way to locate information in a passage. In this text, the first sentence of paragraph 4 signals that the paragraph will talk about the characteristics of a planet. Reread the paragraph and look for details that compare dwarf planets to planets.

STOP!

ⓒommon ⓒore ELA
STANDARDS

RL.3.1
Ask and answer questions to demonstrate understanding of a text, referring explicitly to the text as the basis for the answers.

RL.3.2
Recount stories, including fables, folktales, and myths from diverse cultures; determine the central message, lesson, or moral and explain how it is conveyed through key details in the text.

RL.3.3
Describe characters in a story (e.g., their traits, motivations, or feelings) and explain how their actions contribute to the sequence of events.

RL.3.7
Explain how specific aspects of a text's illustrations contribute to what is conveyed by the words in a story (e.g., create mood, emphasize aspects of a character or setting).

Read this passage and then answer the questions that follow.

Freddy's Way

1 When the clock struck eleven, Freddy turned from the window where he had been watching for nearly an hour and he said: "Guess Dan has forgotten to come for me. I think I'd better write a letter to Mother." His aunt, whom he was visiting, answered:

2   "That will be a sensible thing to do, dear."

3   Freddy worked very hard on his letter. When it was finished, he said: "It doesn't look as nice as it might, but I guess Mother will know I tried to do my best." His aunt replied:

4   "I'm sure she will; anyway, the main thing was to keep your promise and write to her."

5   Presently, Freddy took his cap and went outdoors to find amusement for himself; it was a beautiful warm day, just the kind when a boy loves to go swimming, and he thought longingly of the river. But his aunt did not wish him to go alone, and for some reason, Dan had failed to call for him. The next-door neighbor was mowing his lawn and Freddy asked: "Need any help?" The man answered:

6   "Sure, I was just wishing for a boy to rake the grass."

7   Freddy set about his work whistling, and the neighbor never guessed that his small helper had had a disappointment that morning. It was Freddy's happy way when he could not do one thing to find another and do that cheerfully.

continued

Name_____ Date_____

Question 1

Look back at the passage and think about Freddy's reaction when he realized that Dan wasn't coming to play with him. What did he say and what did he choose to do?

1. This question has two parts. Answer Part A first. Then answer Part B.

Part A What lesson can be learned from "Freddy's Way"?

A Do not try to do too much at once.

B Whatever you do, do it with all your might.

C People should learn to make the best of a situation.

D Always treat others the way you want to be treated.

Part B What sentence from the passage supports your answer to Part A?

A The next-door neighbor was mowing his lawn and Freddy asked: "Need any help?"

B Freddy set about his work whistling, and the neighbor never guessed that his small helper had had a disappointment that morning.

C When it was finished, he said: "It doesn't look as nice as it might, but I guess Mother will know I tried to do my best."

D Presently, Freddy took his cap and went outdoors to find amusement for himself; it was a beautiful warm day, just the kind when a boy loves to go swimming, and he thought longingly of the river.

Name_____ Date_____

2. What can you tell from the illustration?

A   the type of house Freddy lives in

B   how the character Freddy feels as he is waiting.

C   what the weather is like

D   what the setting of the story is

3. Choose four words that best describe Freddy in "Freddy's Way." Check the box next to each word you choose.

☐   careless

☐   responsible

☐   helpful

☐   dreamer

☐   lazy

☐   cheerful

☐   shy

☐   selfish

☐   friendly

Question 2

When answering multiple-choice questions, try to eliminate, or cross out, any answers that you know are not true.

Question 3

Think about Freddy's actions during the story. How did Freddy react when Dan didn't come by? Did he keep his promise to his mother? What did he offer to do after he wrote the letter? What do these actions tell you about Freddy?

continued

Name_____ Date_____

Question 4

At the beginning of the story, the reader finds out that Freddy is waiting for his friend Dan, but the answer to this question comes later in the story. Reread paragraph 5 to find details to support your answer.

4. Where was Freddy hoping to go at the beginning of the story and why couldn't he go without Dan? Use details from the story to support your answer.

_____

_____

_____

_____

_____

_____

_____

_____

Common Core ELA STANDARDS

RI.3.1
Ask and answer questions to demonstrate understanding of a text, referring explicitly to the text as the basis for the answers.

RI.3.2
Determine the main idea of a text; recount the key details and explain how they support the main idea.

RI.3.6
Distinguish their own point of view from that of the author of a text.

Read this passage and then answer the questions that follow.

A Doggone Delicacy

1   Few things seem as American as going to a baseball game and eating a hot dog. In fact, Americans eat over nine billion hot dogs every year! But did you know that hot dogs were invented in Europe? Or that nobody is certain who came up with the term "hot dog"? So grab some ketchup and mustard. Here are some fast facts about this fast-food favorite.

2   Sausages have been around for centuries. Simply put, a sausage is ground meat with some sort of covering around it. The modern hot dog is a type of sausage that was created in Germany or Austria. In the 1800s, German immigrants came to America and sold hot dogs. Back then they called them "dachshund sausages." (Dachshunds are long, skinny dogs that look like sausages.) The overseas snack became very popular in the United States. Before long, vendors were wandering down the streets selling the tasty treat.

continued ➤

3   Americans quickly put their own spin on the hot dog by adding toppings. People from Michigan put chili, mustard, and onion on their hot dogs. Kansas City hot dogs have sauerkraut (pickled cabbage) and Swiss cheese. Southwestern hot dogs might be topped with jalapeños, salsa, or green peppers—talk about a *really hot* dog!

4   Hot dogs are sometimes called "frankfurters." Frankfurt is a city in Germany that claims to be the birthplace of the hot dog. In 1986, they celebrated the five hundredth anniversary of the hot dog. Austrians from the city of Vienna, which is also called Wien, disagree. That's where we get the term "wiener."

5   Wherever they originated, hot dogs are now a part of everyday American life. And in the 1920s, America even added to the sausage's long history. By dipping hot dogs in cornmeal batter and frying them, Americans created a new dish: the corn dog.

Name_____ Date_____

1. This question has two parts. Answer Part A first. Then answer Part B.

Part A What is the main idea of "A Doggone Delicacy"?

A Even though they were invented in Europe, Americans eat hot dogs more than any other food.

B No one knows where the hot dog came from, but Americans have certainly adopted hot dogs as their own.

C Americans started topping hot dogs with many different types of foods and they even created a hot dog dipped in batter.

D European hot dogs were called many different names throughout history, including wieners, frankfurters, and dachshund sausages.

Question 1
This question is asking you to find the main idea or what this passage is mostly about. Read each of the answer choices and ask yourself: Is this mostly what the passage is about or does it describe just one part of the passage?

Part B What sentence from the passage best supports your answer to Part A?

A In fact, Americans eat over nine billion hot dogs every year!

B Frankfurt is a city in Germany that claims to be the birthplace of the hot dog.

C People from Michigan put chili, mustard, and onion on their hot dogs.

D Wherever they originated, hot dogs are now a part of everyday American life.

continued →

Name_____ Date_____

Question 2

Signal words in a text can help you identify the sequence of events. Words such as *first, next,* and *finally* can signal to the reader the sequence of events. In this passage, the writer uses dates to let the reader know when events happened.

2. Identify the sequence of events in the history of the hot dog, according to "A Doggone Delicacy." Number the events in the order in which they happened.

—　Frankfurt or Vienna invented hot dogs.

—　German immigrants sold dachshund sausages in America.

—　People make sausage by putting ground meat inside a covering.

—　Americans invented corn dogs by frying batter-dipped hot dogs.

3. What were hot dogs called when they first arrived in America?

A　wieners

B　corn dogs

C　frankfurters

D　dachshund sausages

Question 3

When you find answer choices that are words directly from the passage, find and underline those words in the text. Then read the sentences right around your underlines to find information just about those words. You can see which words best answer the question.

Name_____ Date_____

4. What is the author's point of view on the invention of hot dogs? Use details from the text to support your answer.

_____

_____

_____

_____

_____

_____

_____

_____

Question 4

The author's point of view is what the author thinks or believes about a topic. Reread paragraph 4. What information does the author tell you about the invention of the hot dog? What does that tell you about the author's point of view? What other statements does the author make about the origins of the hot dog?

Common **C**ore **ELA**
STANDARDS

RL.3.2
Recount stories, including fables, folktales, and myths from diverse cultures; determine the central message, lesson, or moral and explain how it is conveyed through key details in the text.

RL.3.4
Determine the meaning of words and phrases as they are used in a text, distinguishing literal from nonliteral language.

RL.3.6
Distinguish their own point of view from that of the narrator or those of the characters.

Read this passage and then answer the questions that follow.

Making New from Old

CHARACTERS:

LI: A young Chinese-American girl

MEI: Li's grandmother, a Chinese-American woman

(*Scene: An open street lined with suburban houses. It is fall, and the weather is cold but bright. A barking dog and a rush of wind can be heard as Li and Mei enter the scene, walking together.*)

1   LI (*anxiously*): Lao Lao,* can we walk faster? My stomach is grumbling.

2   MEI: All right, Li, I will try to keep up with you. (*takes a deep breath*) I like to stroll along this street and enjoy the beautiful scenery during daylight hours, especially in autumn when the leaves are fiery in the trees and crisp beneath our feet.

3   LI: Is that the reason you read at your window bench each afternoon, to catch the last bit of sun before the evening swallows it up?

*Lao Lao is a Chinese word for grandmother.

4   MEI (*thoughtfully*): I suppose so. Look ahead! (*pointing*) What is that by the side of the road, in front of the blue house?

5   LI: It looks like (*pausing*) . . . I think it's an ugly old garden bench, left outside.

6   MEI: Come, let's go and see it. What does the sign say? I've forgotten my eyeglasses—read it for me, Li.

7   LI: It says "Free." (*dismissively*) Just somebody's unwanted furniture, Lao Lao. Come on! There are colorful fall trees ahead! (*begins to walk more quickly, passing the bench*)

8   MEI: Wait, Li. (*stops walking*) Consider this bench with me.

9   LI (*sighing impatiently and returning to stand with Mei near the bench*): What about it, Lao Lao? It's sad-looking, all worn out and cracked in places. Plain old broken stuff isn't any use to us.

10   MEI: Oh, certainly, it's faded and needs repair, but imagine what it could be with a bit of sanding and some new paint. You could design a window bench for yourself, like mine.

11   LI (*suddenly interested*): You think so? Will you teach me to make those improvements? I was just telling Mom how I dreamed of having my own window bench.

12   MEI: I'm glad, Li. People these days call it "upcycling," making something new out of something worn and neglected but still good. All you need is patience and an eye for hidden potential. We'll call your father to help carry this, and we'll upcycle it together.

13   LI (*eagerly*): And then, just like you, I can sit by the window's light, enjoying the day until it creeps below the horizon.

14   (*They sit together on the bench while Mei begins dialing Li's father on her cell phone.*)

continued

Name_____ Date_____

Question 1

When you are trying to figure out an unknown word, read around the word for clues. These clues are called "context clues" and can be a definition, or even synonyms or antonyms of the word. Read the sentences around the unknown word to figure out its meaning.

1. This question has two parts. Answer Part A first. Then answer Part B.

Part A Read the sentence from "Making New from Old."

> I like to <u>stroll</u> along this street and enjoy the beautiful scenery during daylight hours, especially in autumn when the leaves are fiery in the trees and crisp beneath our feet.

What does the word <u>stroll</u> mean?

A to limp ahead

B to walk slowly

C to move softly

D to step quickly

Part B Which phrase from the passage helps you understand what the word <u>stroll</u> means?

A I will try to keep up with you

B enjoy the beautiful scenery

C you read at your window bench

D Li and Mei enter the scene, walking together

Name_____ Date_____

2. Identify the phrases that show Li's point of view and the phrases that show Mei's point of view. Put a checkmark in the correct box beside each piece of information.

Phrase	Li's Point of View	Mei's Point of View
I dreamed of having my own window bench.	☐	☐
It's an ugly old garden bench.	☐	☐
Let's go and see it.	☐	☐
Broken stuff isn't any use to us.	☐	☐
Imagine what it could be with a bit of sanding.	☐	☐
We'll upcycle it together.	☐	☐
Enjoying the day until it creeps below the horizon.	☐	☐

Question 2
Point of view is a character's attitude or way of thinking about things. Understanding a character's point of view helps you understand that character much better.

continued

Name_____ Date_____

Question 3

Sometimes authors tell a story or write a passage to give readers a message and to make them think about something. What is this author trying to make you think about?

Question 4

When you retell a story, you only want to include the most important points. To answer this question, make a list of the three most important events in this story. Then use the list to write your response.

3. What is the author's message in "Making New from Old"?

A Old furniture should be put by the side of the road.

B Grandmothers can teach their grandchildren many things.

C A window bench is perfect for reading and sitting in the sun.

D Something that looks old might be recycled into something new.

4. Retell "Making New from Old" in your own words.

_____

_____

_____

_____

_____

_____

_____

_____

ommon
ore ELA
STANDARDS

RI.3.2
Determine the main idea of a text; recount the key details and explain how they support the main idea.

RI.3.3
Describe the relationship between a series of historical events, scientific ideas or concepts, or steps in technical procedures in a text, using language that pertains to time, sequence, and cause/effect..

RI.3.4
Determine the meaning of general academic and domain-specific words and phrases in a text relevant to a *grade 3 topic or subject area*.

RI.3.6
Distinguish their own point of view from that of the author of a text.

Wind turbines like these generate electricity from the wind.

Read this passage and then answer the questions that follow.

Energy: The Science of Making Things Happen

1   Energy is essential for life. Living things need energy to run, leap, think, and even sleep. Nonliving things that work, like machines, phones, and cars, also use energy. Energy is the part of nature that does work.

2   For living creatures, energy comes mostly from food. Eating well helps our bodies do things. This energy keeps us warm and helps our brains, hearts, and muscles work.

continued ➡

3   For nonliving things like machines, energy comes differently. Trains, computers, and vacuum cleaners can't eat food as living things do. Instead, their energy comes from the earth's resources. Some of these resources, like gas and coal, can be used up. These nonrenewable resources are taken from the earth for electricity and other types of energy. After they are used, they can't be used again. In addition, burning coal and oil is bad for the environment. They cause air and water pollution. This is not good for our world.

4   Are there better sources of energy for machines? After all, machines are important for our lives. Doctors use them to help people, children use them to learn, and friends use them keep in touch. Thankfully, there are ways to use machines without hurting our world. Some energy resources are renewable. Energy from the sun, and even from running water and wind, can be used for the same kinds of things gas and coal are used for. These are better because they can't be used up.

5   Renewable energy resources like the sun and wind won't run out because there will always be sunshine and windy days. Those resources are also cleaner for our environment. They do not cause air and water pollution. With some smart and creative thinking about energy, we can keep it around to help people do things for many years to come.

Name_____ Date_____

1. This question has two parts. Answer Part A first. Then answer Part B.

Part A What is the meaning of the word <u>essential</u> as it is used in this passage?

A basic

B necessary

C helpful

D harmful

Question 1

Try replacing the word *essential* with each of the answer choices listed. Ask yourself: Does this word fit in this sentence? Does the meaning of the sentence stay the same?

Part B Which detail from the passage helps you understand the meaning of the word <u>essential</u>?

A living things need energy

B nonliving things that work

C energy is the part of

D to run, leap, think

continued

Name_____ Date_____

Question 2

Think of what happens because of each cause listed in the chart. For example: Machines need energy to work, so _____. Which of the effects in the chart best completes that idea?

2. Based on the passage, choose the cause of each effect listed. Draw a line connecting the cause to the effect.

Cause

Machines need energy to work.

People need energy to move and think.

Gas and coal are nonrenewable sources of energy.

The sun and wind are renewable resources.

Effect

They get energy from resources in the earth.

They get energy from the food they eat.

After they are used, they are gone.

Energy from the sun and wind are better for the environment.

Name_____ Date_____

3. What is the author's point of view on the different sources of energy? Use details from the text to support your answer.

_____

_____

_____

_____

_____

_____

_____

Question 3

To answer this question, reread the text and look for places where the author has stated an opinion. For example, in paragraph 3, the author states an opinion about nonrenewable energy. What other opinions can you find? The opinions will help you identify the author's point of view on the topic.

continued ➡

Name_____ Date_____

Question 4

To answer this question, first go back to the passage and underline the sentences that explain why living things need energy and why nonliving things need energy. Then use the information for your answer.

Start your answer by turning the question into the first sentence of your answer: Energy is essential for life because_____.

4. Explain why energy is essential for life. Use details from the text to support your answer.

_____

_____

_____

_____

_____

_____

_____

_____

_____

STOP!

Read the passage. Then answer questions 1–10.

A New World

1   Home is like a dream these days, Palma thought. She remembered her village on the Philippine island of Panay with a dull ache. That was home. She had lived near Tapaz, where the palm trees grew wild and the weather was either muggy and warm or rainy. People rode motorbikes to get around, sometimes with a whole family piled aboard one bike. Shops and homes were open and inviting. No one wore long-sleeved shirts. The smell of cook smoke hung in the air, as did the fragrance of flowers. Friends and family laughed and played together in the evenings.

2   Then Palma moved to Minneapolis, Minnesota, where everything was strange. People lived all crammed together in a loud, bustling, tall city. They seemed to rush all the time, driving about in large cars. Ads flashed colorful pictures, music played, buses honked, and traffic lights changed over and over (red, green, yellow, red, green, yellow in a never-ending cycle).

continued ➤

3   Palma and her grandmother had left Tapaz in October to live with her aunt and uncle, who had moved to Minneapolis many years before. The village had been at its hottest when they left. Insects buzzed all the time, and people stayed inside during the scorching afternoons.

4   It was so different here! The weather was cold—colder than Palma had ever known. The air was like the inside of a refrigerator. Her breath was frosty in the mornings. She had to wear heavy coats and scarves, and still her nose and the tips of her ears got cold. Palma often stayed inside where it was warm, watching her favorite movie over and over again. It was about the Chinese heroine Mulan, whose father was getting old. Mulan pretended to be a boy so she could join the army in her father's place.

5   One afternoon the sky clouded over completely, and it grew even colder. Palma pointed at the sky and asked Aunt May, "What's happening?"

6   Aunt May laughed. "You'll see, *mija*."

7   The clouds seemed to hang lower, and the sky grew darker as Palma watched from the window. The heater ticked on often. She was grateful for its warmth. Just when Palma thought the sky would burst, white flakes began to fall from above.

8   "Auntie!" Palma cried in surprise.

9   Aunt May came in from the kitchen and looked out the window. She smiled. "Ah, now it is time. Come along."

10   Together, they bundled up in their warm clothes and walked out of the apartment to the sidewalk. By now, the white flakes were drifting down faster and thicker. Palma had never seen anything like it! She held out her hand, and a flake landed in the center of her palm. It was so small and light that she did not feel it until it melted.

11   "What is it called?" she asked.

12   "Snow," Aunt May answered. "It happens when rain gets very cold and freezes in the sky. Then it falls to Earth as soft, delicate flakes. Sometimes so many flakes fall that the snow piles up on the ground, and it might stay there all winter."

13   They watched the snow for several quiet minutes. People rushed about on the street as usual. None of them seemed to think the snow was strange. Palma made a little whining noise. Her eyes welled with tears.

14   "What is it, *mija*?" Auntie asked.

15   "I don't like it here. It is cold and strange, and now we have snow. I miss my friends and my village. I want to go home."

16   Auntie was quiet for a moment, thinking. Then she said, "I know that it is hard to move to a new place. It was hard for me, too. Remember the story of Mulan, though. She was brave and courageous for the good of her family. Your family lives here now. Can you be brave and courageous for us, too?"

17   Palma thought about it. "Yes," she decided finally, "I can do that."

18   She and Aunt May stood and watched the snow for a bit longer before they went back inside. The snow was falling faster, and it made everything seem quiet and peaceful. This new world was still strange to her, but she decided that it could be beautiful as well.

continued

Name_____ Date_____

1. This question has two parts. Answer Part A first. Then answer Part B.

Part A Read this sentence from paragraph 13.

Palma made a little whining noise.

Why did Palma make a whining noise?

A   She was upset.

B   She was hurt by the snow.

C   She was practicing her English.

D   She was copying the sound of people rushing by.

Part B Which sentence from the passage supports the answer to Part A?

A   They watched the snow for several quiet minutes.

B   People rushed about on the street as usual.

C   None of them seemed to think the snow was strange.

D   Her eyes welled with tears.

Name_____ Date_____

2. This question has two parts. Answer Part A first. Then answer Part B.

Part A Read this sentence from the passage.

> People lived all crammed together in a loud, <u>bustling</u>, tall city.

What is the meaning of the word <u>bustling</u>?

A noisy

B busy

C large

D boring

Part B Choose two phrases from the passage that help you understand the meaning of the word <u>bustling</u>.

A all crammed together

B driving about

C rush all the time

D red, green, yellow

E colorful pictures

3. Why didn't Palma like living in Minneapolis?

A She thought the people there were always angry.

B She wanted to move to a city in a different state.

C She was used to living in a village that was very different.

D She was worried that she would have to return to her home.

continued ▶

Name_____ Date_____

4. How does Palma change by the end of the story? Check the box for the three details that tell what she is like at the end.

☐ She no longer misses her village in the Philippines.

☐ She has learned to accept the idea of snow.

☐ She will make the best of her new home for the sake of her family.

☐ She is going to forget about her friends back in the Philippines.

☐ She will stop watching movies on TV and start playing outside more.

☐ She realizes that things that seem strange at first can also be beautiful.

5. How did Palma copy the actions of the Chinese girl Mulan?

A She decided to act for the good of her family.

B She decided to run away from home.

C She joined the army in her father's place.

D She started packing to get ready to return home.

Name_____ Date_____

6. Choose three sentences from the passage that show how Palma
felt about being in Minneapolis. Check the box next to each of your
answers.

❑   Home is like a dream these days, Palma thought.

❑   Then she moved to Minneapolis, Minnesota, where everything was
     strange.

❑   Together, they bundled up in their warm clothes and walked out of
     the apartment to the sidewalk.

❑   Aunt May came in from the kitchen and looked out the window.

❑   The weather was cold—colder than Palma had ever known.

❑   Auntie was quiet for a moment, thinking.

continued ➡

Name_____ Date_____

7. Choose three things Palma noticed about Minneapolis that were different from her home in the Philippines. Check the box next to each thing you choose.

☐   The smell of cook smoke hung in the air.

☐   The palm trees grew wild.

☐   The air was like the inside of a refrigerator.

☐   The heater ticked on often.

☐   Whole families rode on motorbikes.

☐   No one wore long-sleeved shirts.

☐   There were buses and traffic lights.

Name_____ Date_____

8. Why did Palma's aunt mention Mulan to her? Use details from the
passage to support your answer.

_____

_____

_____

_____

_____

_____

9. As the snow is falling, what does Auntie see when she looks at Palma?
Describe Palma at that moment from Auntie's point of view. Include at
least two details from the passage.

_____

_____

_____

_____

_____

_____

continued ➡

Name_____ Date_____

10. What lesson does Palma learn in this story, and how does she learn it?
Use at least three details from the passage to support your answer.

_____

_____

_____

_____

_____

_____

_____

_____

_____

_____

_____

_____

Common Core Reading Warm-Ups & Test Practice Grade 3 • ©2014 Newmark Learning, LLC

A View of the Bombardment of Fort McHenry, by J. Bower, 1816.

Read the passage. Then answer questions 1–10.

The Story of the Star-Spangled Banner

1   Mary Pickersgill made her living sewing flags. Over the years she stitched many flags. In 1813, Major George Armistead needed a new flag and gave the job to Mary. He asked that it be "so large that the British will have no difficulty in seeing it from a distance." The flag was to fly over Fort McHenry in Baltimore, Maryland. Mary did not know it, but her flag would become the most famous flag in U.S. history.

A Battle in the War of 1812

2   The United States and Great Britain were at war while Mary worked on the flag. After the flag was finished and hung at the fort, the British marched into Washington, D.C. They set fire to the White House and the Capitol building. Next, they turned to the nearby port city of Baltimore. For a day and a night, British warships fired on Fort McHenry.

continued ➤

3   The battle could be seen for miles. A young American watched all through the night from a distant ship. That man, Francis Scott Key, was still awake at dawn. The big flag was still flying over Fort McHenry! And British ships were leaving the city.

A Song Full of Pride

4   Filled with joy and pride in his country, Key wrote a song about what had happened. First he called it "The Defense of Fort McHenry." Later he changed the name. The new name is "The Star-Spangled Banner." Every American should know the song as our national anthem.

A Family Treasure

5   When the war was over, Major Armistead kept the flag. After his death, his wife, daughter, and grandson cared for it. The family kept the flag for 90 years. From time to time, they put it on display in Baltimore.

6   Meanwhile, Key's song about the flag became well known. More people heard about the flag. More people wanted to see it. Bits of the flag were cut off and given away as souvenirs. Sixty years after the battle, the flag was wearing out. At that time, Armistead's grandson was the flag's owner. He wanted it to be preserved. In 1912, he gave the big flag to the American History Museum. The museum is part of the Smithsonian Institution in Washington, D.C.

A National Treasure

7 Today the flag is on display at the Smithsonian. It is kept safe behind glass under low light. The big flag known as the "stars and stripes" belongs to all Americans. You can visit the flag in Washington, D.C. You can visit it online, too, at the Smithsonian's website. There, you can see the flag and zoom in on details. You can learn about the missing star, the writing on the flag, and more. Like millions of others, you can enjoy this national treasure.

Broad Stripes and Bright Stars

8 The first lines of Francis Scott Key's song describe the sight of the flag's "broad stripes and bright stars." The stripes *were* broad, and each star was fully two feet wide! The flag was huge: thirty feet high and forty-two feet wide. It had fifteen stars and fifteen stripes for the thirteen colonies plus Vermont and Kentucky. Mary Pickersgill and four young helpers worked on the flag ten hours a day for six weeks. Pickersgill was paid $405.90 for her work.

continued

Name_____ Date_____

1. In what part of the passage can you read about the attack on Fort McHenry?

A the first paragraph

B A Battle in the War of 1812

C A Song Full of Pride

D A National Treasure

2. This question has two parts. Answer Part A first. Then answer Part B.

Part A According to the passage, why was the flag created?

A Mary Pickersgill wanted to become famous.

B The Smithsonian was looking for a large flag to display.

C The British had attacked Fort McHenry.

D Major Armistead needed a flag for Fort McHenry.

Part B Which part of the passage gives details that support the answer to Part A?

A the first paragraph

B A Song Full of Pride

C A National Treasure

D Broad Stripes and Bright Stars

Name_____ Date_____

3. This question has two parts. Answer Part A first. Then answer Part B.

Part A Read this sentence from the passage.

> At that time, Armistead's grandson was the flag's owner. He wanted it to be <u>preserved</u>.

What is the meaning of the word <u>preserved</u>?

A shared with others

B kept from harm

C repaired or fixed

D hidden from sight

Part B Choose each detail from the passage that helps you understand the meaning of <u>preserved</u>. Check the box next to each detail you choose.

☐ The flag was wearing out.

☐ The family gave the flag to the American History Museum.

☐ Bits of the flag were cut off and given away.

☐ The flag was displayed in Baltimore from time to time.

☐ That man, Francis Scott Key, was still awake at dawn.

continued

Name_____ Date_____

4. You can tell that the author of this passage believes that

A Major Armistead was a good leader.

B Mary Pickersgill knew Francis Scott Key.

C the Armistead family still owns the flag.

D the flag is an important part of our nation's history.

5. In the last part of the passage, the author refers to a website. Why does the author want readers to visit the site? Check the box next to your answer choices.

☐ to zoom in on the flag's details

☐ to meet Mary

☐ to sing "The Star-Spangled Banner"

☐ to enjoy a national treasure

☐ to visit Washington, D.C.

☐ to see what the big flag looks like

☐ to write their name on the flag

Name_____ Date_____

6. What details does the illustration show about Fort McHenry and the battle? Check the box next to each detail you choose.

☐ A lot of people lived close to the fort.

☐ The fort was surrounded by water.

☐ Many British ships took part in the attack.

☐ The armies fought with rifles.

☐ No one was hurt in the battle.

☐ The attack came from the sea.

☐ The battle ended before nightfall.

7. Read these sentences from the passage. Choose two sentences that express the author's point of view. Check the box next to each sentence you choose.

☐ The United States and Great Britain were at war while Mary worked on the flag.

☐ Next, they turned to the nearby port city of Baltimore.

☐ Mary did not know it, but her flag would become the most famous flag in U.S. history.

☐ Every American should know the song as our national anthem.

☐ In 1912, he gave the big flag to the American History Museum.

continued

Name_____ Date_____

8. Explain how the flag got from Fort McHenry to the Smithsonian
Institution in Washington, D.C. Use details from the passage in your
answer.

_____

_____

_____

_____

_____

_____

_____

Name_____ Date_____

Common Core Reading Warm-Ups & Test Practice Grade 3 • ©2014 Newmark Learning, LLC

9. Explain how many stars and stripes were on the flag that flew at Fort McHenry and what they stood for.

_____

_____

_____

_____

_____

_____

_____

continued

Name_____ Date_____

10. Why does the author call Pickersgill's flag a "national treasure"? Give
details from the passage to support your response.

_____

_____

_____

_____

_____

_____

_____

_____

_____

_____

_____

_____

_____

_____

Read the passages. Then answer questions 1–10.

Robbie's Dragon

1   Robbie and Lena lay on a blanket looking up at the sky and waiting for shooting stars. Every few minutes, a meteor shot across the sky.

2   "That meteor looks like a falling dragon," Robbie said.

3   "Everything looks like a dragon to you," Lena teased. "Your stuffed bunny looks like a dragon. I bet even that new lizard you have looks like a dragon to you."

4   Robbie took his pet lizard out of his pocket. It was a leopard gecko named Harry. Robbie rubbed Harry's belly. He could almost imagine sparks coming from the lizard's nose.

5   "Yup. If it was colder out, Harry would be breathing fire!" Robbie teased.

6   Lena answered, "Little brothers are so weird."

7   Robbie yawned and leaned back on the blanket to watch the stars. He was really sleepy.

continued ➡

8   The next thing Robbie knew, he was trying to feed Harry. But it seemed like Harry had grown enormously overnight. By the end of the day, he was as large as a cat. A day later, he was the size of a big dog. Robbie's parents wouldn't let him keep a lizard as big as that! Robbie kept Harry hidden in his room. He sneaked scraps from dinner so Harry wouldn't be hungry.

9   Things were soon getting out of hand. One day, Harry was so hungry that he tried to eat Robbie's favorite toy bunny. Even worse, when Harry slept, fire shot out from his nostrils. It scorched Robbie's pillow, leaving small burn marks. Then Robbie noticed a pair of small wings growing on Harry's back.

10   Robbie stood up on his toes and held onto Harry's shoulders. He tried to look Harry in the eye. "You're not really a gecko, are you?" he asked.

11   Harry shook his head sadly.

12   "You're really a dragon, right?"

13   The dragon nodded.

14   "You must miss your family."

15   The dragon nodded several times.

16   "Okay, let's see if we can help you find them," Robbie said. He led the way outside.

17   It was a clear, dark night. Thousands of stars twinkled overhead.

18   The dragon had never flown before, but he raised his wings, and slowly lifted his body into the air. He was so happy that fire shot out of his mouth.

19   "Be careful," Robbie said. "Don't start a fire!"

20   The dragon landed on the ground, looking embarrassed.

21   "Do you know where your family is?" Robbie asked. The dragon nodded.

22   "Then go find them," Robbie said as the dragon just stood there. "Go," Robbie said again, pointing toward the sky.

23   Slowly, the dragon raised his wings. Higher and higher he
flew, spitting bursts of fire. Before long, he was no more than
a bright, tiny ball of light, racing across the sky.

24   Lena suddenly shook Robbie. "Hey, sleepyhead, it's past
your bedtime. We should go back in the house. And don't
forget your lizard."

25   Robbie rubbed his eyes and looked at the stars. For a
moment, he wasn't sure where he was. He thought he saw
Harry winking at him from a great height. Then he patted the
small warm bundle in his shirt pocket. "Wow, that was weird,"
he said to himself.

continued

Moe's Discovery

1   "Come on, Moe," Marley called to her dog. "Let's have an adventure!"

2   Moe looked up at Marley. He had been napping comfortably for nearly an hour. Now he could tell that a good thing must come to an end. Slowly he rose from the ground and obeyed Marley.

3   "That's the boy!" Marley smiled, putting on his leash.

4   The pair walked toward Marley's parents, who were busy unpacking the car and setting up the campsite. Everyone in the family was happy to be back at their favorite spot for a week of camping. Marley's younger brother sat at the picnic table, playing with his toy cars.

5   "Mom, Moe and I are going to take a walk down to the lake," said Marley.

6   "That's fine, dear." Marley's mother smiled at her and then looked over at Marley's father.

7   Marley's father nodded and said, "I could use a walk; I'll go with you."

8   Marley, her dad, and Moe started out on the curvy trail. Along the way, Moe sniffed at the bushes. He smelled the rocks. He padded along in the dirt, following each step Marley took. Then suddenly, he stopped in his tracks.

9   "What is it, boy?" asked Marley. She stopped and waited for Moe. He sniffed the ground excitedly and began to whine. "What do you smell?" Marley asked, watching Moe for some kind of an answer.

10   Marley bent down and began closely examining the ground. "I don't see anything," she said to her dad. Then she tugged on Moe's leash. "Come on, Moe," she urged. But Moe didn't budge. Instead, he started to bark.

11   "Moe!" Marley scolded. "What is your problem?" Moe looked up, confused. Then he barked some more. "Dad, what is he doing?" Her dad shrugged and looked at Moe.

12   "All right, all right—show us!" On hearing Marley's command, Moe began to dig. Dirt flew behind him and he kept digging. Then Moe pulled something out of the dirt. Marley saw something red in Moe's mouth. He dropped it on the ground and panted hard. Marley picked it up in amazement.

13   "Moe, you found Martin's toy fire truck! He was so unhappy last year when he lost it! Come on! Let's go bring it back!" Moe seemed to nod and bounded off with Marley and her father toward the camp.

14   "Martin, look what Moe found!" Marley shouted. Martin jumped up and ran to Moe, smothering him with hugs. Moe enjoyed the attention. It seemed that he knew exactly what he was doing.

15   "There's just one weird thing. I wonder how it got there in the first place?" Marley asked out loud. Moe panted happily. For a second, it almost looked like the dog gave her a wink.

continued

Name_____ Date_____

1. Which sentence **best** tells the important events in the story "Robbie's Dragon"?

A Robbie sees shooting stars in the sky and thinks they could be dragons.

B Robbie's pet lizard grows really fast and does things that prove it is really a dragon.

C Robbie discovers that his lizard is a real dragon and sends it home to its family.

D Robbie falls asleep while stargazing and dreams that his pet lizard is a dragon.

2. This question has two parts. Answer Part A first. Then answer Part B.

Part A What does the word <u>scorched</u> mean in paragraph 9?

A slept

B burned

C folded

D melted

Part B Which phrase from paragraph 9 helps you understand the meaning of <u>scorched</u>?

A when Harry slept

B fire shot out

C from his nostrils

D Robbie's pillow

Name_____ Date_____

3. What can you tell about the story "Robbie's Dragon" from the illustration?

A The story has a very sad ending.

B The story describes some scary events.

C The story tells about something that could not really happen.

D The story tells about real children and their pets.

4. This question has two parts. Answer Part A first. Then answer Part B.

Part A Which event takes place before the story begins?

A Lena gets a pet dragon.

B Lena feeds Harry his dinner.

C Robbie gets a pet lizard.

D Robbie falls asleep on a blanket outdoors.

Part B Which detail from the passage supports the answer to Part A?

A Harry grows bigger than Robbie.

B Robbie already has Harry in his pocket.

C Lena teases her brother.

D Lena calls her brother sleepyhead.

continued ➤

Name_____ Date_____

5. Which four details should go into a retelling of "Moe's Discovery"?
Choose the four details and number them in the correct order.

—   Moe digs up a toy fire truck.

—   Martin is playing with toy cars at the picnic table.

—   Marley wakes Moe up from his nap.

—   Marley, her father, and Moe go for a walk.

—   Marley, her father, and Moe bring the fire truck back to Martin.

—   Marley and her family are camping at their favorite spot.

6. Read this sentence from "Moe's Discovery."

But Moe <u>didn't budge</u>.

What does the phrase <u>didn't budge</u> mean in this sentence?

A to sit quietly

B to not move

C to not change thoughts

D to not care about something

Name_____ Date_____

Common Core Reading Warm-Ups & Test Practice Grade 3 • ©2014 Newmark Learning, LLC

7. In what ways are the characters Marley and Robbie alike? Check the box next to each answer you choose.

- ☐ They both have siblings.
- ☐ They both like camping.
- ☐ They both take care of animals.
- ☐ They both have imaginary friends.
- ☐ They are both ten years old.
- ☐ They are both kind to their pets.

continued

Name_____ Date_____

8. What makes Robbie think that Harry is really a dragon? Use details from the passage to explain.

_____

_____

_____

_____

_____

_____

Name_____ Date_____

9. In "Robbie's Dragon," does the author provide any hints to the reader
that Robbie is dreaming? Use details from the text to support your
answer.

_____

_____

_____

_____

_____

_____

_____

continued →

Name_____ Date_____

10. Both "Moe's Discovery" and "Robbie's Dragon" include characters that deal with animals. What can the reader tell about Marley and Robbie based on how they act toward their animals?

_____

_____

_____

_____

_____

_____

_____

_____

_____

_____

_____

_____

Read the passages. Then answer questions 1–10.

Native American Tribes of Georgia

1   Long before Columbus reached America, Native Americans were settling across the country. They farmed, hunted, and carved out villages in the wilderness. In the southeast, there were two large Native American tribes: the Cherokee and the Creek.

2   The Cherokee tribe was spread out across what is today Georgia and Alabama. In total, it took up an area of 100,000 square miles! The Cherokee tribe grew so large because it invited other people to join them. Native Americans from other tribes, European settlers, and former slaves were welcome in the Cherokee Nation. Within the Cherokee Nation there were seven different clans, and each clan had a different job. The *Aniwaya*, or "Wolf Clan," for example, served as the army. The "Paint Clan" (*Aniwodi*) served as doctors. The "Deer Clan" (*Anikawi*) could run very fast and were skilled hunters.

3   The Cherokee were not nomadic hunters. They mostly stayed in one place. They lived in houses made of mud and clay and wore clothing made from animal skin. One thing they had that many tribes did not was a written language. A man named Sequoyah was a Cherokee silversmith who developed a *syllabary*. Unlike the alphabet, the syllabary was a collection of between eighty-four to eighty-six different syllables. These syllables were rearranged to make up Cherokee words.

continued

4   The Creek tribe had the largest population of any tribe in Georgia until the 1760s. The tribe's name came from English settlers living in South Carolina who often traded with them. Since the Native Americans lived near the Ochese Creek, the settlers called them "Creeks." The name stuck. The Creek tribe was friendly to the English colonists. They even helped them establish a colony in Savannah. Savannah later became the first state capital of Georgia. The Creeks were skilled hunters and traded deerskins for metal, cloth, and other textiles. Like the Cherokee, Creeks invited outsiders to become citizens of their tribe.

5   The Creek lived in houses made out of grass or river cane, which is a kind of bamboo. Before Western influence, they wore clothing fashioned from plants or animal hides. Even bark was used to make clothing! Similar to the Cherokee tribes, they too had clans, including Bear, Deer, and Fish.

6   Sadly, the Creek and Cherokee tribes were forced off of their land in the 1800s. Many Native Americans traveled west to Oklahoma and continued their traditions there. Today, the state government recognizes the Creek and Cherokee as the only American Indian tribes of Georgia.

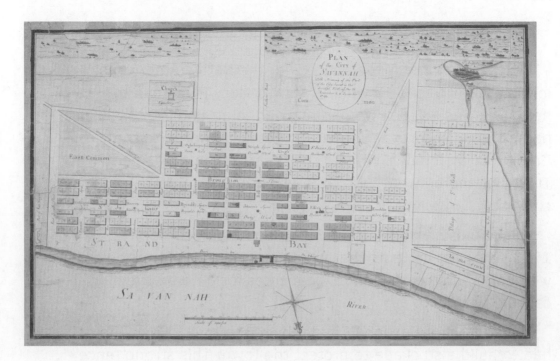

Courtesy of Library of Congress

First Settlers of Savannah

1   On a chilly morning in November of 1732, 114 people boarded a ship in England called the *Anne*. The group included men, women, and children. They were embarking on an adventure that would change their lives. They were sailing to America to found the new colony of Georgia.

2   Almost two months later, in 1733, they arrived in South Carolina. However, that was not their final stop. Their leader, James Edward Oglethorpe, had work to do first. He traveled south along the coast to find a good home for the colonists.

3   Oglethorpe found an ideal place for the settlement. Other countries such as Spain wanted this land, so Oglethorpe chose a place on a hill. It was called Yamacraw Bluff. Being up high would protect the colonists from attack. Also, the site was surrounded by swamps, which would slow down any attackers.

continued

4   Next, Oglethorpe made peace with the Native Americans in the area. He asked a woman named Mary Musgrove to help. She was a Creek woman married to an Englishman named John Musgrove. She introduced Oglethorpe to the Creek leader, Tomochichi, and they reached an agreement. Then Oglethorpe went back to South Carolina to gather his colonists.

5   The colonists arrived at their new home on February 1, 1733. They set up tents that would protect them from the weather. Then they began to clear trees for a home they called Savannah.

6   The settlers of Savannah had a huge job to do. First, they had to build a stockade to protect the town. This strong fence was made with logs. Then the settlers had to build homes for everyone. When spring came, they planted crops.

7   Savannah was the first planned city in America. That means people designed the city before it was built. The plan divided the city into twenty-four parts. Each part would have a square in the center. These squares would be meeting places for merchants and neighbors. By 1734, four of these squares had been built.

8   These first colonists had many different skills. There were tailors, gardeners, and carpenters. There was one *wheelwright*, *potash* makers, a *turner*, a *miller*, and a baker. There were also *mercers* who planned to sell silk. Silk was a popular fabric at the time, but it was very expensive. Silk is produced by silkworms, which feed on the leaves of the mulberry tree. The British believed that the climate in Georgia was perfect for growing mulberry trees and developing a silk industry. So the colonists began to grow mulberry trees.

9   However, not everyone was suited to the hard work. Not everyone liked to farm. The silkworms did not grow well in the Georgia climate, so silk production was not a great success.

10   People's health suffered, too. Pure water was hard to find. Disease-carrying insects from the swamps bit the colonists, and many became sick. In the first year, many colonists died. Others left Georgia and went back to South Carolina, where the living was easier.

11   Despite the hardships, more people arrived in Savannah in the next few years. The climate was great for cotton, and the farmers began growing it instead of trying to make silk. Some of the people made fortunes from selling cotton and other crops. They began to build fancy homes near the town squares. Savannah became a nice place to live.

12   Today, you can visit Savannah and see twenty-one of the original squares. You can walk along the streets shaded by oak trees and see the grand homes. You can stand on Yamacraw Bluff. With a little imagination, you can picture what it was like for the first people who settled in this beautiful place.

Glossary

mercer: a person who trades or sells fine cloth and fabrics

miller: a person who grinds grains to make flour

potash: a substance made from wood ashes and used as a fertilizer for plants

turner: a person who cuts or shapes wood with a machine

wheelwright: a person who makes wheels

continued

Name_____ Date_____

1. Read the sentence from "Native American Tribes of Georgia."

> The Creeks were skilled hunters and traded deerskins for metal, cloth, and other <u>textiles</u>.

What does the word <u>textiles</u> mean?

A arrows

B animals

C fabric

D seeds or food

2. This question has two parts. Answer Part A first. Then answer Part B.

Part A According to "Native American Tribes of Georgia," how were the Cherokee and the Creek Native Americans alike?

A They both helped the colonists form cities.

B They both lived in houses made out of mud.

C They both welcomed outsiders into their tribes.

D They both made clothing out of plants and animal skin.

Part B Which sentence from the passage supports your answer to Part A?

A They even helped them establish a colony in Savannah.

B Like the Cherokee, Creeks invited outsiders to become citizens of their tribe.

C Before Western influence, they wore clothing fashioned from plants or animal hides.

D They lived in houses made of mud and clay and wore clothing made from animal skin.

Common Core Reading Warm-Ups & Test Practice Grade 3 • ©2014 Newmark Learning, LLC

Name_____ Date_____

3. Read the list of details from "Native American Tribes of Georgia" in the chart below. What was the effect of each of these? Match the effect to its cause. Write the correct answer in the chart.

Cause	Effect
The Cherokee allowed outsiders into their tribe.	
The Creek were skilled hunters.	
The tribe used things found in nature.	
The tribe lived by water.	

A They had animal skins to trade.

B The tribe grew larger.

C The settlers gave them the name "Creek."

D They wore clothing made from plants and bark.

continued

Name_____ Date_____

4. This question has two parts. Answer Part A first. Then answer Part B.

Part A Who was most important in making the new colony at Savannah a success?

A Tomochichi

B Mary Musgrove

C John Musgrove

D James Oglethorpe

Part B Which two details from the passage support the answer to Part A? Click on the details you choose.

☐ James Oglethorpe chose a place that was protected from attacks.

☐ John Musgrove was married to Mary Musgrove, a Creek woman.

☐ Tomochichi signed an agreement with the settlers.

☐ Mary Musgrove introduced Oglethorpe to Tomochichi.

☐ James Oglethorpe worked to make peace with the Creek Indians.

Name_____ Date_____

5. Choose two reasons the early settlers in Savannah had hard times. Check the box next to each answer you choose.

☐ They built twenty-four squares in the first year.

☐ Native Americans attacked them.

☐ Pure water was hard to find.

☐ They could not find any silkworms.

☐ Not everyone liked to farm or work hard.

6. What tasks did the settlers complete after they arrived in Savannah? Choose the five tasks and number them in order.

— They built a stockade.

— They cleared the land.

— They boarded a ship.

— They planted crops.

— They sailed to America.

— They built homes.

— They set up tents.

continued

Name_____ Date_____

7. Read each piece of information in the chart. Decide whether the information is included in "Native American Tribes of Georgia" or "First Settlers of Savannah." Put a checkmark in the correct box beside each piece of information. If the information appears in both passages, check both boxes.

Information	Native American Tribes of Georgia	First Settlers of Savannah
The Creek helped establish an English colony in Savannah.	☐	☐
The English talked with the Creek leader about the land.	☐	☐
The Creek invited outsiders into their tribe.	☐	☐
The Creek were pushed off their land.	☐	☐
Savannah had a hard beginning, but it soon became a good place to settle.	☐	☐
The English gave the tribe the name "Creek."	☐	☐
An Englishman was married to a Creek woman named Mary Musgrove.	☐	☐

Name_____ Date_____

8. In "Native American Tribes of Georgia," what is the author's point of view about the Cherokee and Creek? Use details from the passage to support your answer.

_____

_____

_____

_____

_____

_____

9. Explain why life was very hard for the first settlers of Savannah. Use details from "First Settlers of Savannah" to support your answer.

_____

_____

_____

_____

_____

continued

Name_____ Date_____

10. Describe the relationship between Native Americans and European settlers. Use details from both "Native American Tribes of Georgia" and "First Settlers of Savannah" in your answer.

_____

_____

_____

_____

_____

_____

_____

_____

_____

_____

_____

_____

_____

Answer Key

Question & Answer	Standards
1 Part A. This question has two parts. Answer Part A first. Then answer Part B. How does Tamika feel about kayaking at the end of the story? A She loves it and wants to go kayaking with Justine every weekend. **B She finds kayaking enjoyable.** C She feels tired and her arms are sore. D She thinks that going kayaking was a mistake.	RL.3.3
1 Part B. Which sentence from the passage supports the answer to Part A? A She could hear Justine telling her to steady her arms and sweep the water. B Within minutes her arms were tired and sore and her feet were getting soaked. **C Tamika suddenly understood how Justine could do this every weekend.** D Although Tamika was moving the kayak better, she was still very tired from the paddling.	RL.3.1
2. What is the author's main message in "Tamika Goes Kayaking"? A Slow and steady wins the race. B Lessons are not given; they are taken. **C Learning something new can be hard, but it is worth it.** D It is important to be careful when trying a new sport.	RL.3.2
3. Read the sentence from "Tamika Goes Kayaking." Once inside, Tamika <u>adjusted</u> the foot pegs and the backrest so they were comfortable. What does the word <u>adjusted</u> mean? **A to move something a bit** B to place items into holes C to carve a place for things D to bend parts to fit together	RL.3.4

Question & Answer	Standards
1 Part A. This question has two parts. Answer Part A first. Then answer Part B. What is the main idea in "Galileo: The Man Who Loved to Learn"? **A Galileo created a new way of learning about the world by testing and trying to prove his ideas.** B Galileo was one of the only people in his time who believed that the Earth moved around the sun. C Galileo was born in Italy and he studied math, stars, and nature so that he could better understand his world. D Many important leaders did not want people to believe Galileo and his ideas because they were afraid of him.	**RI.3.2**
1 Part B. Which sentence from the passage supports your answer to Part A? A He was even forced to stay inside his house, and never leave, for a few years. B He studied math, the stars, and nature. C Because many of Galileo's ideas were new, some powerful leaders were against him. **D Though other people had thought of these things, Galileo was the first person who did work to provide proof.**	**RI.3.2**

Question & Answer	Standards
2. Based on the passage, match each cause to its effect. Draw a line from the cause to the effect.	**RI.3.3**

Cause	Effect
Galileo loved learning.	He proved that the sun did not move around the Earth.
Galileo didn't just want to read books; he wanted to test his ideas.	He studied nature, math, and philosophy.
Galileo studied the planets and sun through a telescope.	He became popular and was considered a great thinker.
Galileo wrote many of his new ideas in books.	Leaders were scared of these ideas and did not want people to read his work.
People learned from Galileo's ideas and discoveries.	He started a new way of thinking and study called science.

Question & Answer	Standards
3. Using the information from the chart and the passage, what inference can you make about Galileo's inventions? **A He created tools that could help him do hands-on tests.** B He was mostly interested in space and how the planets moved. C He read every book on a subject before forming a new thought. D He was more interested in inventing new tools.	**RI.3.7**

Question & Answer	Standards
1 Part A. This question has two parts. Answer Part A first. Then answer Part B. Which of the following best describes the poem's form? A Two of the stanzas are the same. B The poem uses rhyming in each stanza. **C The stanzas get longer and build on ideas.** D Each stanza in the poem has the same number of syllables.	**RL.3.5**
1 Part B. What line might the poet have used to begin a seventh stanza? A And in the nest there was a bird B And on the twig there was a leaf C And on the bird there was a raindrop **D And on the feather there was a bug**	**RL.3.5**
2. In which phrase does the poet talk about an object as if it were a person? A Bird in the egg, egg in the nest B Feather on the bird, bird in the egg C Nest on the branch, branch on the tree **D Tree on the hill, and the hill stood still**	**RL.3.4**
3. What is the central message in "Tree on the Hill"? A Birds build their nests in trees. B Animals with feathers lay eggs. **C Everything in life is connected to something else.** D People should treat trees and animals with respect.	**RL.3.2**

Question & Answer	Standards
1 Part A. This question has two parts. Answer Part A first. Then answer Part B. What do red worms need to live and grow? A water pools **B damp bedding** C strong sunlight D freezing temperatures	RI.3.1
1 Part B. Which sentence from the passage supports your answer to Part A? A Pick a new spot each time you add food. B Cover the bin with plastic or a tarp during freezing weather. **C Make sure the bedding is kept very moist, like a sponge.** D Use a wooden or plastic bin or other nonmetal container.	RI.3.1
2. Choose three sentences that would be included in a summary of "Making Good Use of Garbage." Number them in the correct order. You have to change their bedding at least once a year. Worms are very good to use for fishing and are good for the Earth, but they do not live long in the wild. [3] They need to be covered with a tarp during cold weather. Make a box using plastic or wood, but be sure to stay away from metal containers. **[1] Vermicomposting is using worms to recycle food waste into plant food.** **[3] Worms can be fed fruits, vegetables, coffee grounds, and bread, but they should not be fed meat, eggs, or milk.** They can live in damp shredded newspaper, sawdust, or leaves. **[2] Worms need a warm, dark place with moist bedding and food so that they can grow.**	RI.3.2
3. Read the sentence from "Making Good Use of Garbage." Their <u>population</u> may double or triple in 1 year. What is the definition of the word <u>population</u>? A the years of life **B the number of beings** C the length of something D the size of a certain space	RI.3.4

Question & Answer	Standards
1 Part A. This question has two parts. Answer Part A first. Then answer Part B. Which of the following words best describes the third man? A lazy **B clever** C selfish D honest	**RL.3.3**
1 Part B. What sentence from the passage supports your answer to Part A? A Eager young men often knocked on his door. **B But the third man stayed up all night to ponder the riddle and came up with an answer.** C Only the correct answer would get the young man to the top. D In the morning, the beans had sprouted into three different things.	**RL.3.3**
2. Read the sentence from the passage. They asked him how to reach the <u>peak</u> of the mountain. What does the word <u>peak</u> mean in this sentence? A a clear path B a hidden cave **C a pointed top** D a smooth side	**RL.3.4**
3. Why did the wise man give out magical beans? **A They were the only way to reach the princess.** B They were a test to see who could answer the riddle. C They were the prize for a correct answer to the riddle. D They were food for the hungry men who came from far away.	**RL.3.1**

Question & Answer	Standards
1 Part A. This question has two parts. Answer Part A first. Then answer Part B. What is the main idea of "What Is Pluto?" A Pluto is now called a dwarf planet because it is much smaller than other space objects. B The universe is so huge that astronomers are always finding new planets and moons. **C Scientists are learning more about objects in the universe and what it means to be a planet.** D The dwarf planet Pluto has five moons that have been discovered with telescopes.	RI.3.2
1 Part B. Which of following details from the text support the main idea? Check the box next to each detail you choose. **Astronomers use telescopes to discover new objects like plutoids.** Pluto has three moons. Charon is about half the size of Pluto. **In 2003, an astronomer saw a new object beyond Pluto.** **Finding Eris caused other astronomers to talk about what makes a planet a "planet."** An astronomer is a person who studies stars and other objects in space.	RI.3.1
2. What is the author's purpose for writing "What Is Pluto?" **A to inform readers about planets and space** B to entertain readers with stories about space C to persuade readers that Pluto is a dwarf planet D to convince readers that Eris is the farthest planet	RI.3.6
3. Read the sentence from "What Is Pluto?" This group decided that Pluto was not really a planet because of its size and <u>location</u> in space. What does the word <u>location</u> mean? A path B time **C place** D Color	RI.3.4
4. Explain how a dwarf planet is similar to a planet and how it is different from a planet. Use details from the text to support your answer. **Sample answer:** A dwarf planet is similar to a planet because it orbits the sun. It is different from planets because of its size and location. The text states that a dwarf planet is so small that it can't clear objects out of its path.	RI.3.2

Question & Answer	Standards
1 Part A. This question has two parts. Answer Part A first. Then answer Part B. What lesson can be learned from "Freddy's Way"? A Do not try to do too much at once. B Whatever you do, do it with all your might. **C People should learn to make the best of a situation.** D Always treat others the way you want to be treated.	RL.3.2
1 Part B. What sentence from the passage supports your answer to Part A? A The next-door neighbor was mowing his lawn and Freddy asked: "Need any help?" **B Freddy set about his work whistling, and the neighbor never guessed that his small helper had had a disappointment that morning.** C When it was finished, he said: "It doesn't look as nice as it might, but I guess Mother will know I tried to do my best." D Presently, Freddy took his cap and went outdoors to find amusement for himself; it was a beautiful warm day, just the kind when a boy loves to go swimming, and he thought longingly of the river.	RL.3.2
2. What can you tell from the illustration? A the type of house Freddy lives in **B how the character Freddy feels as he is waiting** C what the weather is like D what the setting of the story is	RL.3.7
3. Choose four words that best describe Freddy in "Freddy's Way." Check the box next to each word you choose. ☐ careless ☑ **responsible** ☑ **helpful** ☐ dreamer ☐ lazy ☑ **cheerful** ☐ shy ☐ selfish ☑ **friendly**	RL.3.3
4. Where was Freddy hoping to go at the beginning of the story and why couldn't he go without Dan? Use details from the story to support your answer. **Sample answer:** Freddy wanted to go swimming but he his aunt didn't want him to go alone because it wasn't safe. The story says that it was the kind of day "a boy loves to go swimming" and that Freddy "thought longingly of the river". The text also states that his Aunt "did not wish him to go alone".	RL.3.3

Question & Answer	Standards
1 Part A. This question has two parts. Answer Part A first. Then answer Part B. What is the main idea of "A Doggone Delicacy"? A Even though they were invented in Europe, Americans eat hot dogs more than any other food. **B No one knows where the hot dog came from, but Americans have certainly adopted hot dogs as their own.** C Americans started topping hot dogs with many different types of foods and they even created a hot dog dipped in batter. D European hot dogs were called many different names throughout history, including wieners, frankfurters, and dachshund sausages.	**RI.3.2**
1 Part B. What sentence from the passage best supports your answer to Part A? A In fact, Americans eat over nine billion hot dogs every year! B Frankfurt is a city in Germany that claims to be the birthplace of the hot dog. C People from Michigan put chili, mustard, and onion on their hot dogs. **D Wherever they originated, hot dogs are now a part of everyday American life.**	**RI.3.1**
2. Identify the sequence of events in the history of the hot dog, according to "A Doggone Delicacy." Number the events in the order in which they happened. Frankfurt or Vienna invented hot dogs. **[2]** German immigrants sold dachshund sausages in America. **[3]** People make sausage by putting ground meat inside a covering. **[1]** Americans invented corn dogs by frying batter-dipped hot dogs. **[4]**	**RI.3.1**
3. What were hot dogs called when they first arrived in America? A wieners B corn dogs C frankfurters **D dachshund sausages**	**RI.3.1**
4. What is the author's point of view on the invention of hot dogs? Use details from the text to support your answer. **Sample answer:** The author's point of view is that hot dogs could have been invented in either Frankfurt or Vienna and that it isn't that important. The author explains how both places claim to be the inventor of the hot dog and that "wherever they originated" they are now American.	**RI.3.6**

Question & Answer	Standards
1 Part A. This question has two parts. Answer Part A first. Then answer Part B. Read the sentence from "Making New from Old." I like to <u>stroll</u> along this street and enjoy the beautiful scenery during daylight hours, especially in autumn when the leaves are fiery in the trees and crisp beneath our feet. What does the word stroll mean? A to limp ahead **B to walk slowly** C to move softly D to step quickly	**RL.3.4**
1 Part B. Which phrase from the passage helps you understand what the word <u>stroll</u> means? **A I will try to keep up with you** B enjoy the beautiful scenery C you read at your window bench D Li and Mei enter the scene, walking together	**RL.3.4**
2. Identify the phrases that show Li's point of view and the phrases that show Mei's point of view. Put a checkmark in the correct box beside each piece of information. If the information appears in both passages, check both boxes.	**RL.3.6**

Phrase	Li's Point of View	Mei's Point of View
I dreamed of having my own window bench.	✔	
It's an ugly old garden bench.	✔	
Let's go and see it.		✔
Broken stuff isn't any use to us.	✔	
Imagine what it could be with a bit of sanding.		✔
We'll upcycle it together.		✔
Enjoying the day until it creeps below the horizon.	✔	

3. What is the author's message in "Making New from Old"? A Old furniture should be put by the side of the road. B Grandmothers can teach their grandchildren many things. C A window bench is perfect for reading and sitting in the sun. **D Something that looks old might be recycled into something new.**	**RL.3.2**
4. Retell "Making New from Old" in your own words. **Sample answer:** Li and her grandmother Mei are taking a walk. Mei sees an old, broken garden bench on the side of the road. Mei wants to repair and reuse the bench. At first, Li thinks the bench is junk, but her grandmother teaches her how to make something beautiful out of something old.	**RL.3.2**

Question & Answer	Standards
1 Part A. This question has two parts. Answer Part A first. Then answer Part B. What is the meaning of the word <u>essential</u> as it is used in this passage? A basic **B necessary** C helpful D harmful	**RI.3.4**
1 Part B. Which detail from the passage helps you understand the meaning of the word <u>essential</u>? **A living things need energy** B nonliving things that work C energy is the part of D to run, leap, think	**RI.3.4**
2. Based on the passage, choose the cause of each effect listed. Draw a line connecting the cause to the effect. **Cause** Machines need energy to work. People need energy to move and think. Gas and coal are nonrenewable sources of energy. The sun and wind are renewable resources. **Effect** After they are used, they are gone. They get energy from resources in the earth. They get energy from the food they eat. Energy from the sun and wind are better for the environment.	**RI.3.3**

Question & Answer	Standards
3. What is the author's point of view on the different sources of energy? Use details from the text to support your answer. **Sample answer:** The author's point of view is that it is better to use renewable resources for energy than nonrenewable resources. The author states that non-renewable resources are "not good for our world" and that renewable resources are "better because they can't be used up." The author also states that sun and wind power are cleaner for the environment.	**RI.3.6**
4. Explain why energy is essential for life. Use details from the text to support your answer. **Sample answer:** Energy is essential for life because both living and nonliving things need energy to work. For example, humans need energy to be able to breathe, run, and think. Machines like cars need energy to make them go.	**RI.3.2**

Question & Answer	Standards
1 Part A. This question has two parts. Answer Part A first. Then answer Part B. Read this sentence from paragraph 13. Palma made a little whining noise. Why did Palma make a whining noise? **A She was upset.** B She was hurt by the snow. C She was practicing her English. D She was copying the sound of people rushing by.	RL.3.3
1 Part B. Which sentence from the passage supports the answer to Part A? A They watched the snow for several quiet minutes. B People rushed about on the street as usual. C None of them seemed to think the snow was strange. **D Her eyes welled with tears.**	RL.3.1
2 Part A. This question has two parts. Answer Part A first. Then answer Part B. Read this sentence from the passage. People lived all crammed together in a loud, <u>bustling</u>, tall city. What is the meaning of the word <u>bustling</u>? A noisy **B busy** C large D boring	RL.3.4
2 Part B. Choose two phrases from the passage that help you understand the meaning of the word <u>bustling</u>. A all crammed together **B driving about** **C rush all the time** D red, green, yellow	RL.3.4

Question & Answer	Standards
3. Why didn't Palma like living in Minneapolis? A She thought the people there were always angry. B She wanted to move to a city in a different state. **C She was used to living in a village that was very different.** D She was worried that she would have to return to her home.	**RL.3.3**
4. How does Palma change by the end of the story? Check the box for the three details that tell what she is like at the end. She no longer misses her village in the Philippines. **She has learned to accept the idea of snow.** **She will make the best of her new home for the sake of her family.** She is going to forget about her friends back in the Philippines. She will stop watching movies on TV and start playing outside more. **She realizes that things that seem strange at first can also be beautiful.**	**RL.3.5**
5. How did Palma copy the actions of the Chinese girl, Mulan? **A She decided to act for the good of her family.** B She decided to run away from home. C She joined the army in her father's place. D She started packing to get ready to return home.	**RL.3.2**
6. Choose three sentences from the passage that show how Palma felt about being in Minneapolis. Check the box next to each of your answers. **Home is like a dream these days, Palma thought.** **Then she moved to Minneapolis, Minnesota, where everything was strange.** **Together, they bundled up in their warm clothes and walked out of the apartment to the sidewalk.** Aunt May came in from the kitchen and looked out the window. The weather was cold—colder than Palma had ever known. Auntie was quiet for a moment, thinking.	**RL.3.3**

Question & Answer	Standards
7. Choose three things Palma noticed about Minneapolis that were different from her home in the Philippines. Check the box next to each thing you choose. The smell of cook smoke hung in the air. The palm trees grew wild. **The air was like the inside of a refrigerator.** **The heater ticked on often.** Whole families rode on motorbikes. No one wore long-sleeved shirts. **There were buses and traffic lights.**	**RL.3.2**
8. Why did Palma's aunt mention Mulan to her? Use details from the passage to support your answer. **Sample answer:** She wanted Palma to make the best of her new situation. Palma was feeling sorry for herself and complaining about her new home. Aunt May compared Mulan giving up her own freedom for her family to Palma's need to help her own family by getting used to a new home.	**RL.3.3**
9. As the snow is falling, what does Auntie see when she looks at Palma? Describe Palma at that moment from Auntie's point of view. Include at least two details from the passage. **Sample answer:** Palma looks sad and lonely. She does not understand snow, and she is cold all the time. She misses her home and does not want to stay here.	**RL.3.6**
10. What lesson does Palma learn in this story, and how does she learn it? Use at least three details from the passage to support your answer. **Sample answer:** Palma moves to Minneapolis, where everything seems strange, and she does not like it. She complains and feels sorry for herself because she is always cold. Then it starts snowing, and she starts to cry. Her aunt reminds her of Mulan and tells her she should be brave for the good of her family. Palma learns that she should make the best of her situation and begins to appreciate her new life.	**RL.3.2**

Question & Answer	Standards
1. In what part of the passage can you read about the attack on Fort McHenry? A the first paragraph **B A Battle in the War of 1812** C A Song Full of Pride D A National Treasure	**RI.3.5**
2 Part A. This question has two parts. Answer Part A first. Then answer Part B. According to the passage, why was the flag created? A Mary Pickersgill wanted to become famous. B The Smithsonian was looking for a large flag to display. C The British had attacked Fort McHenry. **D Major Armistead needed a flag for Fort McHenry.**	**RI.3.3**
2 Part B. Which part of the passage gives details that support the answer to Part A? **A the first paragraph** B A Song Full of Pride C A National Treasure D Broad Stripes and Bright Stars	**RI.3.1**
3 Part A. This question has two parts. Answer Part A first. Then answer Part B. Read this sentence from the passage. At that time, Armistead's grandson was the flag's owner. He wanted it to be <u>preserved</u>. What is the meaning of the word <u>preserved</u>? A shared with others **B kept from harm** C repaired or fixed D hidden from sight	**RI.3.4**

Question & Answer	Standards
3 Part B. Choose each detail from the passage that helps you understand the meaning of <u>preserved</u>. Check the box next to each detail you choose. **The flag was wearing out.** The family gave the flag to the American History Museum. **Bits of the flag were cut off and given away.** The flag was displayed in Baltimore from time to time. That man, Francis Scott Key, was still awake at dawn.	**RI.3.1**
4. You can tell that the author of this passage believes that A Major Armistead was a good leader. B Mary Pickersgill knew Francis Scott Key. C the Armistead family still owns the flag. **D the flag is an important part of our nation's history.**	**RI.3.6**
5. In the last part of the passage, the author refers to a website. Why does the author want readers to visit the site? Check the box next to your answer choices. **to zoom in on the flag's details** to meet Mary to sing "The Star-Spangled Banner" **to enjoy a national treasure** to visit Washington, D.C. **to see what the big flag looks like** to write their name on the flag	**RI.3.5**
6. What details does the illustration show about Fort McHenry and the battle? Check the box next to each detail you choose. A lot of people lived close to the fort. **The fort was surrounded by water.** **Many British ships took part in the attack.** The armies fought with rifles. No one was hurt in the battle. **The attack came from the sea.** The battle ended before nightfall.	**RI.3.7**

Question & Answer	Standards
7. Read these sentences from the passage. Choose two sentences that express the author's point of view. Check the box next to each sentence you choose. The United States and Great Britain were at war while Mary worked on the flag. Next, they turned to the nearby port city of Baltimore. **Mary did not know it, but her flag would become the most famous flag in U.S. history.** **Every American should know the song as our national anthem.** In 1912, he gave the big flag to the American History Museum.	RI.3.6
8. Explain how the flag got from Fort McHenry to the Smithsonian Institution in Washington, D.C. Use details from the passage in your answer. **Sample answer:** Major Armistead had purchased the flag for Fort McHenry, and he kept it after the war. When he died, the flag was passed to his wife, his daughter, and his grandson. After 90 years, the flag was wearing out. Armistead's grandson gave it to the Smithsonian so it could be preserved.	RI.3.3, RI.3.1
9. Explain how many stars and stripes were on the flag that flew at Fort McHenry and what they stood for. **Sample answer:** Mary Pickersgill placed fifteen stars and fifteen stripes on the flag. Thirteen stars and stripes stood for the original thirteen colonies (which became states). The other two stood for the states of Vermont and Kentucky.	RI.3.5, RI.3.1
10. Why does the author call Pickersgill's flag a "national treasure"? Give details from the passage to support your response. **Sample answer:** The author calls the flag a national treasure for many reasons. First, it was the flag that flew over Fort McHenry during an important battle in the War of 1812. Second, it was really big and could be seen from far away. It showed onlookers that the Americans still held the fort. Third, the flag inspired Francis Scott Key to write a song. The song, called "The Star-Spangled Banner," became our national anthem. Fourth, the flag is on display in Washington, D.C., for all Americans to see.	RI.3.2, RI.3.1

Question & Answer	Standards
1. Which sentence **best** tells the important events in the story "Robbie's Dragon"? A Robbie sees shooting stars in the sky and thinks they could be dragons. B Robbie's pet lizard grows really fast and does things that prove it is really a dragon. C Robbie discovers that his lizard is a real dragon and sends it home to its family. **D Robbie falls asleep while stargazing and dreams that his pet lizard is a dragon.**	**RL.3.2**
2 Part A. This question has two parts. Answer Part A first. Then answer Part B. What does the word <u>scorched</u> mean in paragraph 9? A slept **B burned** C folded D melted	**RL.3.4**
2 Part B. Which phrase from paragraph 9 helps you understand the meaning of <u>scorched</u>? A when Harry slept **B fire shot out** C from his nostrils D Robbie's pillow	**RL.3.1**
3. What can you tell about the story "Robbie's Dragon" from the illustration? A The story has a very sad ending. B The story describes some scary events. **C The story tells about something that could not really happen.** D The story tells about real children and their pets.	**RL.3.7**

Question & Answer	Standards
4 Part A. This question has two parts. Answer Part A first. Then answer Part B. Which event takes place before the story begins? A Lena gets a pet dragon. B Lena feeds Harry his dinner. **C Robbie gets a pet lizard.** D Robbie falls asleep on a blanket outdoors.	RL.3.5
4 Part B. Which detail from the passage supports the answer to Part A? A Harry grows bigger than Robbie. **B Robbie already has Harry in his pocket.** C Lena teases her brother. D Lena calls her brother sleepyhead.	RL.3.1
5. Which four details should go into a retelling of "Moe's Discovery"? Choose the four details and number them in the correct order. Moe digs up a toy fire truck. **[3]** Martin is playing with toy cars at the picnic table. Marley wakes Moe up from his nap. Marley, her father, and Moe go for a walk. **[2]** Marley, her father, and Moe bring the fire truck back to Martin. **[4]** Marley and her family are camping at their favorite spot. **[1]**	RL.3.2
6. Read this sentence from "Moe's Discovery." But Moe <u>didn't budge</u>. What does the phrase <u>didn't budge</u> mean in this sentence? A to sit quietly **B to not move** C to not change thoughts D to not care about something	RL.3.4
7. In what ways are the characters Marley and Robbie alike? Check the box next to each answer you choose. **They both have siblings.** They both like camping. **They both take care of animals.** They both have imaginary friends. They are both ten years old. **They are both kind to their pets.**	RL.3.3

Question & Answer	Standards
8. What makes Robbie think that Harry is really a dragon? Use details from the passage to explain. **Sample answer:** Robbie loves dragons and thinks he sees them everywhere. He takes his pet lizard from his pocket. Lena teases him about the lizard being a dragon just before he falls asleep and starts dreaming. In his dream, the lizard grows fast, starts breathing fire, and grows wings.	RL.3.3
9. In "Robbie's Dragon," does the author provide any hints to the reader that Robbie is dreaming? Use details from the text to support your answer. **Sample answer:** The author does include hints to show that Robbie is dreaming. The first hint is when Robbie yawns and leans back on the blanket to watch the stars. The second hint is when Lena shakes Robbie awake.	RL.3.3
10. Both "Moe's Discovery" and "Robbie's Dragon" include characters that deal with animals. What can the reader tell about Marley and Robbie based on how they act toward their animals? **Sample answer:** Both Robbie and Marley are kind people who care about animals. In "Moe's Discovery," Marley loves her dog and even when she is not happy that he won't listen, she is gentle with him. She is excited and proud that he found her brother's truck and she lets Moe know that she is pleased. In "Robbie's Dragon," Robbie is careful with his little gecko, keeping him safely in a pocket so he won't get hurt. In his dream, he takes care of the dragon by feeding it and letting it free to find its family so it will be happy.	RL.3.3, RL.3.9

Question & Answer	Standards
1. Read the sentence from "Native American Tribes of Georgia." The Creeks were skilled hunters and traded deerskins for metal, cloth, and other textiles. What does the word <u>textiles</u> mean? A arrows B animals **C fabric** D seeds or food	**RI.3.4**
2 Part A. This question has two parts. Answer Part A first. Then answer Part B. According to "Native American Tribes of Georgia," how were the Cherokee and the Creek Native Americans alike? A They both helped the colonists form cities. B They both lived in houses made out of mud. **C They both welcomed outsiders into their tribes.** D They both made clothing out of plants and animal skin.	**RI.3.1**
2 Part B. Which sentence from the passage supports your answer to Part A? A They even helped them establish a colony in Savannah. **B Like the Cherokee, Creeks invited outsiders to become citizens of their tribe.** C Before Western influence, they wore clothing fashioned from plants or animal hides. D They lived in houses made of mud and clay and wore clothing made from animal skin.	**RI.3.1**

Question & Answer	Standards
3. Read the list of details from "Native American Tribes of Georgia" in the chart below. What was the effect of each of these? Match the effect to its cause. Write the correct letter in the chart.	RI.3.8

Cause	Effect
The Cherokee allowed outsiders into their tribe.	B
The Creek were skilled hunters.	A
The tribe used things found in nature.	D
The tribe lived by water.	C

A   They had animal skins to trade.
B   The tribe grew larger.
C   The settlers gave them the name "Creek."
D   They wore clothing made from plants and bark.

Question & Answer	Standards
4 Part A. This question has two parts. Answer Part A first. Then answer Part B. Who was most important in making the new colony at Savannah a success? A Tomochichi B Mary Musgrove C John Musgrove **D James Oglethorpe**	RI.3.2

Question & Answer	Standards
4 Part B. Which two details from the passage support the answer to Part A? Click on the details you choose. **James Oglethorpe chose a place that was protected from attacks.** John Musgrove was married to Mary Musgrove, a Creek woman. Tomochichi signed an agreement with the settlers. Mary Musgrove introduced Oglethorpe to Tomochichi. **James Oglethorpe worked to make peace with the Creek Indians.**	**RI.3.1**
5. Choose two reasons the early settlers in Savannah had hard times. Check the box next to each answer you choose. They built twenty-four squares in the first year. Native Americans attacked them. **Pure water was hard to find.** They could not find any silkworms. **Not everyone liked to farm or work hard.**	**RI.3.3**
6. What tasks did the settlers complete after they arrived in Savannah? Choose the five tasks and number them in order. They built a stockade. **[3]** They cleared the land. **[1]** They boarded a ship. They planted crops. **[5]** They sailed to America. They built homes. **[4]** They set up tents. **[2]**	**RI.3.8**

Question & Answer	Standards

7. Read each piece of information in the chart. Decide whether the information is included in "Native American Tribes of Georgia" or "First Settlers of Savannah." Put a checkmark in the correct box beside each piece of information. If the information appears in both passages, check both boxes.

RI.3.1

Information	Native American Tribes of Georgia	First Settlers of Savannah
The Creek helped establish an English colony in Savannah.	✔	
The English talked with the Creek leader about the land.		✔
The Creek invited outsiders into their tribe.	✔	
The Creek were pushed off their land.	✔	
Savannah had a hard beginning, but it soon became a good place to settle.		✔
The English gave the tribe the name "Creek."	✔	
An Englishman was married to a Creek woman named Mary Musgrove.		✔

8. In "Native American Tribes of Georgia," what is the author's point of view about the Cherokee and Creek? Use details from the passage to support your answer.

RI.3.6

Sample answer: The author seems to respect and admire the Cherokee and the Creek. This is shown by the details he or she chose to include and how the details are presented. For example, readers learn that the Cherokee welcomed a wide range of outsiders, including former slaves and Europeans. We also learn that the Creek helped European settlers form a colony. In addition, the author uses the word "sadly" when talking about the tribes' loss of their land.

9. Explain why life was very hard for the first settlers of Savannah. Use details from "First Settlers of Savannah" to support your answer.

RI 3.1

Sample answer: First, the settlers spent two months on a boat crossing the ocean to get to South Carolina. They finally arrived in America and set up tents. They had to live in tents while they worked hard building houses and walls for protection. Many people died from disease or left to return to South Carolina.

Question & Answer	Standards
10. Describe the relationship between Native Americans and European settlers. Use details from both "Native American Tribes of Georgia" and "First Settlers of Savannah" in your answer. **Sample answer:** The Creek and Cherokee tribes lived in the area where the English settlers wanted to build Savannah. James Edward Oglethorpe was the leader of the colony. He met with the Creek leader, Tomochichi. Tomochichi said they could settle on the Creek's land. The Creek let outsiders join their tribe and were friendly with the English. They even helped the English settlers build their colony of Savannah.	RI.3.3